**Praise for *Food Court Druids, Cherohonkees,
and Other Creatures Unique to the Republic***

"Another funny and strangely insightful contribution to our culture from
Robert Lanham, the Margaret Mead of the North American weirdo."

—Neal Pollack, author of *Never Mind the Pollacks: A Rock and Roll Novel*
and *The Neal Pollack Anthology of American Literature*

Praise for *The Hipster Handbook*

"Your offical guide to the language, culture,
and style of hipsters young and old."

—*The Los Angeles Times*

"What *The Preppie Handbook* did for whale belts and synonyms
for vomiting, *The Hipster Handbook* accomplishes for this
generation's stylistic and linguistic signs and signifiers."

—*The New York Times Book Review*

"Describes everything cool . . . in pitch-perfect detail. This guy clearly has
some insider information himself. Gently teasing and hilarious."

—*Philadelphia Weekly*

"Almost embarrassingly funny."

—*Library Journal*

"*The Hipster Handbook* is so comprehensive and so well done that only
a poseur could criticize it without tongue in cheek."

—*Slate*

A page from an Idiosyncrologist's notebook

Also by Robert Lanham
THE HIPSTER HANDBOOK

Food Court Druids, Cherohonkees,

and Other Creatures Unique to the Republic

Robert Lanham

ART BY **JEFF BECHTEL**

A PLUME BOOK

PLUME
Published by the Penguin Group
Penguin Group (USA) Inc., 375 Hudson Street, New York, New York 10014, U.S.A.
Penguin Group (Canada), 10 Alcorn Avenue, Toronto, Ontario, Canada M4V 3B2
(a division of Pearson Penguin Canada Inc.)
Penguin Books Ltd, 80 Strand, London WC2R 0RL, England
Penguin Ireland, 25 St Stephen's Green, Dublin 2, Ireland (a division of Penguin Books Ltd)
Penguin Group (Australia), 250 Camberwell Road, Camberwell, Victoria 3124, Australia
(a division of Pearson Australia Group Pty Ltd)
Penguin Books India Pvt Ltd, 11 Community Centre, Panchsheel Park, New Delhi – 110 017, India
Penguin Books (NZ), Cnr Airborne and Rosedale Roads, Albany, Auckland, New Zealand
(a division of Pearson New Zealand Ltd)
Penguin Books (South Africa) (Pty) Ltd, 24 Sturdee Avenue, Rosebank, Johannesburg 2196, South Africa

Penguin Books Ltd, Registered Offices: 80 Strand, London WC2R 0RL, England

First published by Plume, a member of Penguin Group (USA) Inc.

First Printing, November 2004
10 9 8 7 6 5 4 3 2 1

CIP data is available.
ISBN 0-452-28562-3

Printed in the United States of America
Set in Helvetica Neue and Akzidenz Grotesk Families

"Who have you decided to become? Make this decision consciously. Make it carefully. Make it powerfully."

—Anthony Robbins, "Outstanding People of the World" recipient and guru to the stars

Contents

A NOTE TO OUR READERS

Throughout this book, there are occasions where masculine pronouns are used in order to avoid the awkward usage of gender-neutral pronoun forms such as his/her, he/she, etc. In order to make up for this semantic bias for the masculine, we have happily agreed to donate a portion of the proceeds from this book to the League of Angry Feminists (LAF) and to refer to God as "the flowering vessel" when visiting our respective places of worship. Thanks for your understanding!

Introduction

Creatures Unique to the Republic:
The Third Journal of Idiosyncrology

Idiosyncrology (ĭd'ē-ō-sĭn-krŏl'ə-jē) **n.** *The study and classification of individuals and groups of individuals based on their distinguishing behaviors and idiosyncrasies.*

Anyone who considers New York *THE* melting pot of the world has probably spent too much time in the Big Apple, oblivious to the diversity found west of the Holland Tunnel, north of the Empire State Building, east of the Brooklyn Bridge, and south of Lady Liberty. Sure, racially speaking New York is less homogeneous than, say, Fishgut, Idaho. But defining diversity on racial terms alone seems a bit antiquated these days. In fact, given the meaningful *behavioral* differences of individuals in any given community, suggesting a location is diverse because it has x number of whites, blacks, Hispanics, and Jews, seems prehistoric. If you don't agree, try bragging about your neighborhood's heterogeneous makeup at your next cocktail party:

> "We have more blacks, Mexicans, and homosexuals than you'd *ever* find in our old neighborhood."

Chances are, announcing over dinner that you have foot rot would be better received.

If you want to encounter true diversity, try spending an afternoon at the Walgreens in Hillsboro, Oregon. Pick up a burger at the Salem County rest stop just off the New Jersey Turnpike. Swing by the Piggly Wiggly superstore in Demopolis, Alabama. Or simply take a look around the office where you work, the school you attend, or the Quick Stop where you pump your gas. In fact, spend half an hour observing the hustle and bustle in almost any public setting in America and you'll encounter dozens of discernible American archetypes. More often than not, their unique social habits and behaviors have little if anything to do with race, religion, or sexual orientation.

Perhaps you'll encounter a **WB**, an individual who really identifies with a *Bugs Bunny* character and wears Warner Bros. clothing exclusively. Or maybe you'll cross paths with a **Cherohonkee**, a white baby boomer who dresses like a Native American. Or perhaps you'll spot a **Yankneck**, whose New Hampshire license plate and Confederate flag bumper sticker are somehow in perfect harmony.

You know these people. You've seen them. You may even *be* one of them. They're all emerging American archetypes.

In the budding field of science known as **Idiosyncrology**, anthropologists compile and document the unique social habits and behaviors of the people who make up the social framework of contemporary society. Having done meticulous field research in food courts, college campuses, offices, and JCPenneys, we explore new ways to classify groups of individuals based on their behavior, dress styles, and means of expression as opposed to their skin color, race, and religious affiliation. In an era when the racial lines drawn by earlier generations have become increasingly murky, it is the Idiosyncrologist's goal to group these emerging archetypes into meaningful categories called *Idio Types* (Idiosyncrological Types).

In the past three years, the field of Idiosyncrology has gained widespread recognition. *The Hipster Handbook* shed light on the ubiquitous genus known as the Hipster. And our introductory academic text, *Cyborgs, Libertarians, and People Who Like Vin Diesel,* was recently adopted by the Texas school board as part of their core, statewide curriculum for high school students. We have even received acclaim from the medical community:

> "If Nora Roberts were to write an academic tome about *Cyborgs, Libertarians, and People Who Like Vin Diesel,* this is *precisely* what it would be like. Watch out, Mrs. Roberts, a new talent has arrived!" says Dr. Phil of Robert Lanham's work.

Idiosyncrology is a humanitarian science that celebrates the role of the individual in society. It is for this reason we use the term "republic," a term derived from the Latin *res publica*, meaning, literally, "public affair." A commonwealth designed by the people. The term has become an antiquated way to refer to the United States, but it's time to reclaim it. America doesn't happen inside the DC beltway, in a courthouse, or on Wall Street. America is a public affair. America is the sound of

Dr. Phil gives Lanham's work a thumbs-up.

diverse voices. America is its people. America is a republic. Without further ado, we present *Food Court Druids, Cherohonkees, and Other Creatures Unique to the Republic.*

How to Use This Book

Most people are already familiar with some of the more fundamental Idio Types, such as Trekkies, Eurotrash, Goths,[1] LaRouche supporters, and, of course, people who say "poon." This book is intended for those advanced readers who possess a formidable understanding of basic Idio Types. (*If you are unfamiliar with these basic types, an introductory tape series narrated by Cokie Roberts is available.*) For each Idio Type included in this study, an **Idio Rank** has been assigned designating overall quirkiness and level of dysfunction (see page 1).

We will also present several one-of-a-kind individuals in a recurring section called **CATSCAN**s (Cannot Attempt to Socially Categorize, Anthropologically Noteworthy). These are individuals whose idiosyncrasies defy classification but warrant proper study to better understand society as a whole.

Since additional Idio Types are discovered daily, it would be too ambitious an endeavor to comprehensively document all of them in one volume. Thanks to a generous grant from the *New England Journal of Science*, our work continues to grow, enriching lives as we slowly begin to better understand the diversity of our world. Please visit us today at foodcourtdruids.com to read about or suggest additional Idio Types.

---

[1] Please refer to our recent article "The Goth Pilgrim: A Case Study" for more information on a new breed of Goths who wear knickers, eighteenth-century attire, and listen to The Cure.

WARNING

You or someone you know
may be included in this study.

Idio Rank Scale

1   normal

2   mildly unusual

3-4   eccentric but socially acceptable

5-6   neurotic, borderline weird

7   very strange, dysfunctional

8   do not trust with children

9   do not trust with scissors

10   run, this person is a freak

The Cube People

Though his intentions were probably benign, Bob Propst's creation of the cubicle is arguably first runner-up to the Razor scooter as the most annoying invention of the twentieth century. Millions if not billions of workers spend the majority of their professional lives working within the constraints of a cube. Simply put, it sucks. Though cost-effective, cubicles strip workers of their privacy, making it challenging to perform essential work tasks such as opening *young slutz taking it hard* e-mail attachments. They also create a safety risk since their walls are too thin to deflect a bullet, should that shifty guy in Accounting with psoriasis become overly disgruntled. If there is a hell, Bob Propst will be sent there. Sentenced to listen to an eternity-long Casio keyboard remix of "Do You Believe in Life After Love?" While he sits in a cube.

Since its creation in 1968, use of the cubicle has become increasingly common. In fact, 60 percent of the white-collar workforce works in cubes. Media saturation is often said to be integral to the shaping of the modern psyche, but until now, **cube saturation** has not been given its proper due. In fact, the loss of personal space in the office has helped spawn a myriad of distinct office personas unique to this time in history. The *Linux* (cranky tech-support guys), and *Drool Tools* (employees who smack their lips and crinkle bags while eating) are some common breeds found in most offices. In part 1 of this book, we will begin our study by discussing some key Idio Types that you may have encountered on the way to the water cooler.

 This image indicates that more thorough research on this particular Idio Type is pending.

1 Happy Mondays

IN BRIEF: Excessively cheerful office workers with overly earnest or maternal natures

POPULATION SIZE: Common

GENDER: Female

HABITAT: Vinyl-siding-friendly neighborhoods

HOBBIES: Reviewing fun movies like *The Other Sister* and *The Full Monty* for the company newsletter

SCREEN SAVER: Kitty cats, puppies, or children

IDIO RANK: 6.8

Overview

She has a candy dish, the contents of which are not dissimilar to what you'd find at your grandmother's house: miscellaneous hard candies, starlight mints, Tootsie Rolls, saltwater taffy, circus peanuts, and generic Reese's knockoffs with peanut butter that's mysteriously crumbly. She's the Happy Monday, an individual as essential to the office experience as paper jams in the copy machine.

Happy Mondays are as warm and giving a people as one could hope to know. They get their name from their relentlessly pleasant temperaments, which, somehow, allow them to be in good spirits even at 7 A.M. on a Monday morning. Happy Mondays are always the first people to arrive in the office. As you pass them on the way to your desk, they're sure to greet you with a playful "here comes trouble" or an animated "happy English muffin hour." Always true to their nurturing instincts, Happy Mondays are sure to inform you that there's fresh coffee and Krispy Kremes in the kitchen.

WARNING: In many cases the aforementioned candy dish is a trap, laid cunningly by the Happy Monday to lure you into talking to her about her children/cat/dog or overactive thyroid.

All Warm and Fuzzy

Most Happy Mondays decorate their desks with pictures of their husbands and tack their children's crayon illustrations to the sides of their cubicles. If you're part of the Happy Monday's inner circle, she'll invite you over to her desk daily to show you Polaroids of family outings to Chuck E. Cheese. And no visit is complete without the full tour of young Billy's impressionistic stick figure drawings. He's talented for his age, she informs you, but sometimes has accidents when he drinks too much soda. Those who aren't quite as close with the Happy Monday shouldn't fret. She'll be sure to send photos of her family via e-mail to the entire company before day's end, signed simply: *hope everyone enjoys these:)*

Happy Mondays who don't have children are often obsessed with their pets instead. They decorate their desks with pictures of their beloved furry friends and save photos of them as desktop wallpaper. Some prefer glamour shots of their dogs and cats wearing dresses or sunglasses.

A Happy Monday's candy dish

When discussing their pets and/or children, Happy Mondays often forget that they're at work and begin speaking in baby talk before snapping out of their trance. Showing off a framed picture of a pet, they often exclaim: "Wook at my wittle baby. Mommy will be home soon to kiss your wittle paws, yes she will, whisker-head."

Those fortunate enough to sit in close proximity to a Happy Monday will be delighted by the smell of her rosy perfume and the sound of her humming throughout the day. Sometimes, the popping and cracking of gum is thrown into the mix to provide subtle texture to her soundscapes.

The Artistic Eye

Since Happy Mondays love to talk, having an assortment of conversation props is helpful to them. Many are into crafts and love to discuss any current knitting projects they're working on. If you win their favor they may even knit you a sweater to wear on casual Fridays. The more artsy Happy Monday may let you take a peek at her collection of hand-painted porcelain bunny rabbits, provided you don't touch them.

In spite of their warm personalities and never-ending supply of knitted sweaters, Happy Mondays are always freezing at work. Thankfully, they're fast learners who quickly teach themselves how to adjust the thermostat to a comfortable ninety degrees.

Happy Mondays take it on themselves to brighten the office with decorative touches. You can bet she's the one who made the angel and devil signs above the hole puncher that say "Holey Paper" and "Unholey Paper," respectively. Like all great art, signs such as these provoke thought in all who come in contact with them: *Are these works trying to generate subversive religion-in-the-workplace pleasure or a paranoid religion-in-the-workplace fear? And what's the thematic significance of the teddy bear T-shirt the angel is wearing?*

You Know There's a Tiger Beneath That Curtainlike Dress

Despite her carefree exterior, the Happy Monday takes her job very seriously. She's sweet as a fig, but if there's a shortage of paper in the copier, she becomes crisp and efficient, relentless in her pursuit of the supply boy, never raising her voice when he's found, but informing him of his error with just a hint of edge in her voice and deadness in her eyes. Should you cross her, doubt not that the generous tours of her California Singing Raisins collection will come to an abrupt halt. But once an issue is resolved, she's all sweetness and rainbows again. Thankfully, given the Happy Monday's pleasant demeanor, conflicts rarely arise.

The one sure way to ruffle her feathers is to use crass language. Happy Mondays would rather mouth the phrase "He's in the bathroom" than say it aloud, and they simply have no tolerance for cursing. They discover early on that the phrase "Oh, for heaven's sake" is versatile, useful, and salty enough for them. And *bullcrap* is a VERY powerful word when something a little edgier is needed.

Curiously, Happy Mondays become visibly upset when the time comes to speak up in meetings, but it's difficult to discern if it's a particular issue that has upset them or the speaking itself. Nevertheless, they're quite comfortable one-on-one and never fail to offer valuable tips like "A new Wendy's opened up next to T.J. Maxx and if you get there before 11 A.M., you can get stuff from the breakfast menu *and* the lunch menu."

Bringing Cheer to All

Few would describe Happy Mondays as overachievers. They're more inter-ested in sharing anecdotes from *Guidepost* magazine than working. Never-theless, they do show some initiative. Commonly, Happy Mondays deem themselves the company or department fire wardens and inform everyone on staff about the appropriate safety measures should a fire ever occur. Others keep the bathroom smelling nice with potpourri.

The Hug Certificate

Happy Mondays try to bring joy to the office by actively wearing holiday buttons and sweaters. And when the award is announced for best outfit on Hawaiian Shirt Day, the Happy Monday is the one to beat. They also try to brighten the office by forwarding fun e-mails to their coworkers. The e-mails always have sub-ject lines like "The Hug Certificate" and contain uplifting messages for everyone:

> > You look like you need a hug.
> > Know why? 'Cause everyone needs a hug!!!!
> > *Click here* for **YOUR** free hug :>
> > Keep the hugs going. . . .
> > Forward this message to ten people who you think need a hug.
> > Help make the world a better place.
> > Join the HUG ARMY now!

Should you click on the link as indicated, you'll be taken to a clunky ani-mated image of a baby with outstretched arms. There will be a slogan at the bottom of the page that says "A smile is a frown upside down." Which, of course, as the Happy Monday will reiterate at some point later in the day, it most certainly is.

SPLITSCREENS (Idio Rank: 3.8)

SplitScreens are multitasking employees proficient at doing several things at once. Especially common at companies with fast Internet connections, SplitScreens can watch C-SPAN streams, talk on the phone, listen to the radio, send instant messages, and read CNN on-line all at once. Some SplitScreens can do all the above while eating breakfast and complaining about the disproportionate amount of work they're unfairly assigned.

 JOHNNY FINGERS (Idio Rank: 7.1)

Feeling a little stressed? Need a massage? Not to worry, Johnny Fingers is on his way. Johnny Fingers can always intuit when a coworker is stressed out and will magically appear to give a two-minute massage to those in need. You don't even need to ask! Johnny Fingers appreciates the soothing power of touch and is always willing to forget his work to provide a little relief. Generally, Johnny Fingers is ambiguously gay and enjoys giving massages to male and female workers alike as a selfless, altruistic gesture. Nevertheless, some have been known to inappropriately use the guise of a massage to get a little closer to a coworker. This type of office masseuse is often called Johnny "Really Creepy" Fingers.

2 | CROWs
(Cornered Rabid Office Workers)

IN BRIEF: The office equivalent of the disgruntled coffee shop employee
POPULATION SIZE: Common
GENDER: Male or female
HABITAT: Bars with happy hours
FAVORITE BOOK: *How to Lose Friends and Alienate People*
SCREEN SAVER: Album covers, ironic unicorns and rainbows
IDIO RANK: 6.8

Overview

Always a force to be reckoned with, CROWs have gained notoriety in the workplace with their tendency to lash out unexpectedly at their colleagues. If the person seated next to you isn't religious, but you hear him muttering "Jesus Christ" under his breath throughout the day, chances are you're sitting next to a CROW.

The source of the CROW's discontent lies in his lack of vocational fulfillment, causing him to become bitter and snarky. CROWs are intelligent underachievers who feel their work environments are suppressive and prevent them from realizing their full creative potential. When discussing their work with strangers, they claim to be poets or playwrights, even if they spent the last nine hours doing data entry on the McFlannery acquisition.

A CROW defying the dress code policy

Despite their short fuses, CROWs are able to successfully juggle work, a dysfunctional relationship, and an active drug habit all at once. Assured of their intellectual superiority, they're quite adept at the art of rolling their eyes, and they enjoy discussing the theory that everyone in the Sales Department is retarded. Other CROWs strategically place copies of *Sir Gawain and the Green Knight* beside elite graduate school applications on their desks to illustrate that their current position is beneath them.

Many CROWS are sarcastic and catch coworkers off guard by labeling their trash cans with "in-box" signs. Some develop imaginary work-related illnesses and claim that the overhead lights don't allow the entry of an adequate number of photons into their retinas. All CROWs send out e-mails at least once a week saying "Contact me on my cell, I will be working from home."

Signs That *You* Are a CROW, Part 1

▶ Your computer password is fuck-this-shit.
▶ Everyone knocks on the nonexistent door to your cube.
▶ You have a rearview mirror on your monitor to alert you of enemy approach.
▶ You spend several hours a day making whispery phone calls to friends describing your coworkers' incompetence.
▶ You spend the last ten minutes of every workday counting down the final six hundred seconds.
▶ You commonly complain that the fluorescent lights will suck the soul from your lifeless body.

Sinking Ships and Rising Tempers

CROWs enjoy spreading paranoia about the company's demise, *e.g., No company as disorganized as this one could possibly stay afloat.* They typically claim to do more work than anyone else and grumble that their last place of employment was much more organized. Nevertheless, much of their time at work is spent listening to MP3s with their heads down on their desks. Others kill time creating the perfect cubicle feng shui, wondering to themselves whether the wealth corner is to the right or left of the pencil sharpener. Most commit several hours a day to debating arrival time with their bosses. They believe that it's perfectly acceptable to arrive at noon as long as they work a little bit late.

Thankfully, most CROWs are content to take out their frustrations on inanimate objects such as computers, telephones, and fax machines instead of their coworkers. Should a bag of Doritos become lodged in the vending machine, it will experience a fury that knows no parallel:

"Holy fucking Christ. Fall. Fall, goddamnit. For the love of god, I hate working here!"

DRY LUMPS (Idio Rank: 5.9)

During the workday, the Dry Lump is the quietest person in the office. She's shy, conventional, professional, and 100 percent business. But give her a couple of drinks at the company picnic and she's ready to lean over a balcony Mardi Gras–style and take her top off for *Girls Gone Wild*. To the Dry Lump, one drop of booze is like a shot of Jekyll's formula, transforming her into a woman who enjoys dancing almost as much as she enjoys talking as loudly as humanly possible. After her *third* cocktail, the Dry Lump usually ends up in the back of someone's Ford Explorer. She'll call in sick the next day, but when she finally returns to work, she'll act as if nothing happened.

Making Contact with a CROW

When coming in contact with a CROW, one should always use caution. Thousands of people are injured by office shrapnel yearly just for making the mistake of being in the line of fire when a CROW's computer crashes. Here are a few suggestions to help mollify a potentially explosive interaction, should you have to approach a CROW at work:

▶ Never address a CROW as *chief, buddy, big guy*, or *sweetie*. Affectionate names will make them feel patronized and on edge.

▶ Never approach them directly with a work question. Instead, carry a prop such as a book or CD to discuss and ease your way into work-related topics.

▶ Comfort CROWs with cooing noises. Sometimes, letting them smell the back of your hand can be helpful.

> **WARNING:** Should the CROW at any time become fidgety, or begin sweating, twitching, or shifting in his chair, excuse yourself to the bathroom and complete your conversation via e-mail. *Your safety should always come first.*

Truth be told, CROWs are profoundly out of place in an office environment due to their misanthropic natures and their disdain of company meetings. Offices where a CROW's attitude is allowed to go unchecked sometimes suffer mass outbreaks of CROW's disease, a condition associated with headaches, fatigue, lewd gesturing, and the pilfering of office supplies. More often than not, the CROW's tenure is cut short when he's caught keying his boss's car or mistakenly sends an instant message to a superior that says "Valerie needs someone to rip her a new asshole."

Signs That *You* Are a CROW, Part 2

▶ You knocked the mood lamp off your desk in a fit of rage.
▶ You spend more time smoking in the stairway than you do at your desk.
▶ You spend the first thirty minutes of every morning staring at your monitor and daydreaming about kicking your boss in the rib cage.
▶ You've strategically placed trash cans, plants, and folder drawers to function as a barricade to your desk.
▶ People commonly wonder if you have Tourette's.

3 | Office Lichens

IN BRIEF: Parasitic employees with no skills of their own who are great at delegating tasks to others

POPULATION SIZE: Somewhat common

GENDER: Male or female

HABITAT: Wet, damp climates that facilitate fungal growth

HOBBIES: Sniffing the air for weakness, Tetris

SCREEN SAVER: An Ivy League alma mater

IDIO RANK: 6.7

Overview

As defined by the *Columbia Encyclopedia*, lichens are "slow-growing plant forms of simple structural appearance, composed of blue-green or green algae and fungi living together in symbiosis." In nature, lichens are most commonly found attached to rocks, slowly performing the function of turning rock into soil. Office Lichens, on the other hand, are found brownnosing the office big dogs, attaching to their sides like an additional slimy appendage. Similar to the parasitic, rock-depleting fungus, Office Lichens help to deplete the company's money by ass-kissing their way to higher salaries.

Lichens have no skills of their own but are great at delegating tasks to others. Not surprisingly, Lichens often face a dilemma when they overdelegate and in effect leave themselves with nothing to do. Everyone is ultimately expendable, so in order to ensure job security, Office Lichens quickly make it their top priority to find creative ways to appear busy and essential. When you approach a Lichen at his desk, he's sure to greet you with a solitary finger in the air indicating he's busy and will be with you in a second. After all, it takes him a moment to close out of Friendster.

Lichens make a point to learn all the keyboard shortcuts and instant message abbreviations, like LOL (laugh out loud) and RTM (read the manual), to really look on the ball. Often, they shine their shoes at their desks to appear detail oriented. When put on the spot to define their role on any given project, they say they're the "point person."

Type 1: The Populist Lichen

The Populist Lichen (PL) usually joins the company as a producer or product manager. Being skills challenged, they take it on themselves to become the office shrink and begin listening to the grievances of coworkers to help facilitate productivity. Of course, facilitating productivity in their case is code for finding distracting ways to keep others from realizing they don't know how to open an e-mail attachment.

The Populist Lichen's plan is really quite clever. They visit their coworkers' desks to inquire whether they are having any "issues" with their current tasks. This places them in a position of power. Moreover, since people are always happy to find someone to whom they can divulge work frustrations, most are delighted to find a confidant. A more hands-on Populist Lichen will even take frustrated coworkers into the conference room to discuss their problems at length, and in effect kill more time. More experienced PLs have learned the value of a well-placed hand on the chin when offering consultation. ·

Populist Lichens ultimately report their coworkers' progress and concerns to their superiors and department heads. PLs, of course, have no idea what they're talking about, but their initiative never fails to impress their bosses. Should the boss ask a follow-up question that a PL doesn't have an answer for, they tilt their heads and say, "Let me get back to you on that."

Type 2: The Uptown Lichen

Uptown Lichens have a very different tactic for moving up the corporate ladder. Instead of trying to appeal to the people around them, they schmooze their way into favor by bragging about their summer homes in the country and pretending everyone else in the office is a serf. Uptown Lichens speak of trendy restaurants with names like The Red Room, where the shellfish *à la nage* is simply divine. They drop the names of celebrities and company power players to imply intimacy: *Donald prefers the spreadsheets to be completed on Thursdays*. They brag of Ivy League educations and quote knowingly from the *New York Times* "Style" section. They boast of their jet-setting lifestyles and evenings spent at the club, though upon close scrutiny it's often revealed that "the club" is Bally Total Fitness. And knowing that an image of power is fundamental to success, they incorporate the phrase "I'm not at liberty to reveal" into their conversations to illustrate their deep understanding of the company secrets and esotery.

Uptown Lichens enjoy creating a sense of panic in others by appearing way too busy to be bothered. Nothing is more enjoyable to them than having you sit in the chair in front of their desk for twenty minutes while they talk on the phone. When they finally hang up, they enjoy saying "I'm really swamped right now, can we touch base later?" before dismissing you.

At their core, both types of Lichens suffer from the paranoid belief that they're incompetent. Well, maybe they're not really all that paranoid. Truth be told, they really are pretty worthless.

HOT SAUCE GUY (Idio Rank: 3.2)

Everybody loves the Hot Sauce Guy. He likes things spicy and always has the Tabasco sauce at his desk to prove it. If you're fortunate enough to have a good Hot Sauce Guy at your office, he'll stock his desk with exotic mixtures from foreign lands, like Singapore Sizzle, Aztec Zinger, and Jalapeño Hal. Hot Sauce Guy doesn't discriminate and will never judge coworkers who borrow his milder potions to sprinkle on their take-out at lunch, but should you be daring enough to up the ante and try something with a little bite, he'll smile approvingly and consider you to be one of his own. Hot Sauce Guy is also very easy to shop for should you be lucky enough to draw his name when Secret Santa time rolls around.

4 | TGIFs

IN BRIEF: The *Maxim*-subscribing office pervert.
POPULATION SIZE: Somewhat common
GENDER: Male
HABITAT: Hovering over your cubicle, local battle of the bands
FAVORITE BOOKS: *Cujo*, *Hammer of the Gods*
SCREEN SAVER: The Jägermeister label
IDIO RANK: 6.9

Overview

TGIFs are office workers who carry a pubescent-level worldview with them into adulthood. As their name suggests, TGIFs live for the weekend and the drunken revelry they associate with it. Like the unwanted neighbor who drops by your home unannounced, TGIFs invite themselves into your cubicle, usually at the most inopportune of times. Always animated story-tellers, they announce their presence by saying "I'm sooo hungover" before offering anecdotes from the night before, which usually involve drinking to excess, staying up late to watch *The Man Show*, and sometimes "bon-ing." In reality, most TGIFs are better equipped to work at the arcade or Home Depot than in an office setting.

The TGIF's preferred time for a drop-by is Monday morning, moments after their coworkers have begun turning on their computers. Given the two-day hiatus of the weekend, there's always a lot of catching up to do. Wasting no time, TGIFs swing by and ask, "Hey, dude, what did you do this weekend?" Those who fail to answer immediately, telling the TGIF that they're too busy to talk, are subjected to long monologues about Pink Floyd laser shows, tailgate parties, Vin Diesel movie recaps, or graphic details about drunk chicks they had sex with in the Chi-Chi's parking lot. Known for possessing an extraordinary amount of foresight when it comes to partying, TGIFs generally begin inquiring about your plans for the upcoming weekend before you've even had your first cup of coffee.

As the day progresses, TGIFs get down to business and move on to more work-related topics. They pop by again on their way outside to have a smoke to discuss what the hot chick in Accounting is wearing or to complain that the new receptionist is a sled dog. *"She's got a nice bod though, I'd hit it."*

Keeping It Cool

In high school and college, TGIFs are (of course) very rowdy and more interested in having fun than achieving academic merit. Nevertheless, they're rarely witty or attractive enough to secure a place for themselves in the upper echelons of popularity. Knowing their limitations, TGIFs align themselves with popular kids from the football team, hallway heartthrobs, or popular class clowns to secure themselves roles as yes men. This clever social maneuver enables the TGIF to become popu-

Ways to Keep a TGIF at Arm's Length

USEFUL DETERRENTS FOR MEN

▶ Casually paraphrase Kierkegaard, Nietzsche, and Hegel during conversations about the Celtics.
▶ Begin packing a lunch for him every day to make him think you're creepy.
▶ Tell him you love women but that every now and then you long for a man's strong hands.
▶ Hang a John Stamos poster in your work area.

USEFUL DETERRENTS FOR WOMEN

▶ Strategically stack bridal magazines on your desk.
▶ Ask him for a donation to NOW.
▶ Pump-fake a harassment suit.
▶ Hang a Tori Amos poster in your work area.

USEFUL DETERRENTS FOR EVERYONE

▶ Decorate your desk with hand-painted Dungeons & Dragons figurines and tell him you're a 15th-level Magic-Using Bard with 78 hit points.
▶ Tell him the Sales guy was looking for him (TGIFs can mingle with the Sales guy for hours).
▶ Tell him you've found Jesus and invite him to a prayer group.
▶ Borrow his Hoobastank CD and refuse to return it.
▶ Send him job leads from Hooters.

lar by association. The relationship is a symbiotic one as TGIFs provide social reinforcement by laughing at the popular kids' jokes and supplying ample high fives.

Entering the Workforce

When looking for jobs, TGIFs seek out large corporations like Capital One or Motorola, where they can blissfully slip beneath the radar. Finding an environment where their performance (or lack thereof) will go largely unnoticed is their primary career ambition. Their more important role in the workplace, as they see it, is to provide levity and to enlighten their coworkers with their knowledge of obscure sexual lingo. TGIFs try to enhance their social presence by smoking weed in their cars during lunch, wearing fluorescent baseball caps, and by telling amusing anecdotes that sometimes involve smelling their fingers.

The Party Animal

TGIFs brighten their cubes with pictures torn from *Maxim*, *Stuff*, and *FHM*. They always live beyond their means, buying sporty cars stocked with expensive stereo equipment. Blasting Creed in the company lot shows the ladies their wild sides.

More resourceful TGIFs pick up extra cash on the side by hanging out in the 7-Eleven parking lot to buy beer for minors. This is also a great way to meet teenage chicks.

Especially conspicuous is the TGIF's use of the word "party." Though many people use the term as a verb these days—"I'm going to party hard this weekend"—TGIFs take things a step further by pointedly using the word as playful response to almost any statement:

> **Coworker**: "I think our department will be changing from the Windows XP platform to Windows XP Professional since it appears to be a more stable operating system with a user-friendly interface."
>
> **TGIF response**: "Party."

Conflicts at Work

TGIFs tend to chuckle whenever the word "intern" is mentioned because they believe it has sexual connotations. Sometimes, this lack of interoffice decorum and their tendency to talk degradingly about women can lead to conflict, especially for TGIFs who work in offices dominated by women. When placed in more gender-sensitive work environments, TGIFs adapt by sending suggestive e-mails, thus avoiding the risk of being overheard by uptight employees. Such e-mails usually include porn links or simple updates informing coworkers that they caught a glimpse of Dianne's panties when she stood up. Telling them to e-mail all non-work-related messages to your private e-mail, man_sack_luv@yahoo.com, will usually help to alleviate the problem.

Love and MILFs[1]

TGIFs fantasize about marrying crazy, sexually experimental women who will be open to inviting their female friends into the bedroom. Nevertheless, most settle for "ball-breakers" and women who desire large families, thus forcing them to settle down in their early thirties and limit their crassness to Tuesday-night poker games. Regardless, TGIFs are never fully tamed. They adapt quite naturally to marriage and, with time, are sure to enlighten the office with tales of hot babysitters, MILFs, and the "strange" they're getting on the side.

Tomb Raiders

The Tomb Raider is a sexually aggressive female version of the TGIF. She swings by your desk first thing in the morning to invite you to go "**tomb raiding**" with her; i.e., walking through the cubicle farm floors looking for hot assistants, temps, and interns to flirt with. More aggressive Tomb Raiders go as far as to wink or drag a seductive tongue across their top teeth should they stumble upon a new temp who's especially cute. Tomb Raiders also enjoy boisterously relating their most recent sexual exploits: "I met this guy last night and was TOTALLY ready to rock him, but he didn't want to do anything but cuddle. He was rebounding or something. Can you imagine that shit?"

 **The Bosses**

Everyone has had to work with a totalitarian boss, a passive-aggressive boss, or a boss who wants to be your buddy. Here are six other common types:

THE NAPOLEDRONE (Idio Rank: 7.5)

A boss with a privileged background who has never had to work for anyone else or be in a role of subordination. Napoledrones overcompensate for their lack of experience by bragging about their private-school educations. They often learn the basics of leadership at an early age by telling the cleaning lady to put some extra elbow grease into it when she's scrubbing the floor. After all, humiliation far outweighs patience when it comes to getting the most from your staff.

THE SUN-E-O (Idio Rank: 4.9)

The Sun-E-O is a boss who functions as the company cheerleader. "Wow, team, your hard work sure paid off. Good work." They use

[1]This is an acronym for Mother I'd Like to Fuck. A popular TGIF term.

catchphrases like "onward and upward" at the end of meetings, sometimes encouraging others to chant along. Sun-E-Os are always sure-footed and careful not to stumble since a scraped knee might expose the android circuitry beneath their company-patented poly-fabric man skin suits.

THE HOMOGENATOR (Idio Rank: 7.1)

Bosses who overcompensate for their incompetence by imposing strict standards on their subordinates. Seating charts, dress code standards, strict arrival/departure policies, and the completion of mindless forms and cover sheets are his forte. Some keep ironing boards in their offices.

THE FAVORCRAT (Idio Rank: 6.7)

Like a parent who gives preferential treatment to a child, Favorcrats think Mary should be able to come in a bit late since she works so hard. And why not pick up those room service charges on her expense report? After all, the way she hums after drinking too much coffee is adorable. Not to mention, her attitude is fantastic. Mike, on the other hand, leaves dirty dishes in the break room sink and he wears those horrible shirts with the different colored collars. He can pay for his own goddamn pencils.

THE BOSSMOSIS (Idio Rank: 7.2)

This label is derived from the term "osmosis" and hints at a boss's uncanny ability to discover creative solutions to problems just by having you around. The Bossmosis is even generous enough to introduce your ideas to his superiors as his own, neglecting of course to give you credit. *See also:* **Osmos-Ass**—*a colleague who steals your ideas and takes credit for your work.*

THE HOVERCRAFT (Idio Rank: 5.9)

A boss who spends the majority of his time hovering over the desks of others out of boredom or to assert dominance. Sometimes, their hovering is an attempt to learn how to perform difficult tasks like computer rebooting or attaching a personal photo in an e-mail. Some Hovercrafts are shape-shifters who can mysteriously appear from thin air to make sure you're using the correct fax cover sheets with the company logo.

5 | Alpha Weasels

IN BRIEF: Backstabbing employees whose inflated ambitions cause people not to like them and sabotages their chances for advancement

POPULATION SIZE: Moderately common

GENDER: Male or female

HABITAT: The conference room, leadership classes at the community college

FAVORITE BOOK: *Leave 'em Tingling with Excitement: The Perfect PowerPoint Presentation*

SCREEN SAVER: The Windows logo

IDIO RANK: 6.8

Overview

Some people wash their hands fifty times a day. Others obsess until 3 A.M. about impressing their boss with the perfect color-coded spreadsheet. If you fall into the latter category, you could be an Alpha Weasel. Alpha Weasels are too consumed by their ambitions to have a life beyond the walls of the office. Their idea of relaxation is curling up next to a warm fire on a chilly night to read the latest data analysis report. For fun, they generate lists of how to outperform a coworker who they feel is a threat to their advancement.

An Alpha Weasel's List of Ways to Improve

1. Bring voice up a notch in meetings.
2. Make pager visible on belt *at all times.*
3. Ask boss "Have you seen Johnny?" when Johnny steps out for lunch.
4. Wear company T-shirt on casual Friday.
5. Bring better cookies.

Alpha Weasels always toe the company line and enjoy playing devil's advocate when controversial decisions are made:

"Well, I agree Jeremy was a hard worker and didn't deserve to get fired, but the world is a tough place and work tenure isn't an inalienable right. You gotta admit that."

Beware the Alpha Weasel

Alpha Weasels are easily identified at the office since they accessorize with telephone headsets and pretend to always be on an important call. Curiously, they insist upon answering even the most mundane of calls using speakerphone, subjecting coworkers to Muzak versions of Christopher Cross hits should they be put on hold by tech support. Assuring that their calls are audible to everyone is a great way to show people that they're team players.

Alpha Weasels are undeniably adept at their jobs, but their cattiness and blinding enthusiasm win them few friends. Coworkers who make the mistake of confiding in Alpha Weasels over lunch are surprised when they're called into their boss's office later that day to discuss the particulars of what was thought to be a confidential conversation.

Weekends Are Miller Time (for the Weak)

Since Alpha Weasels are obsessed with their careers, they often alienate their friends outside the workplace. This works to their advantage since they're introverts who prefer staying at home anyway. To the Alpha Weasel, nothing is more satisfying on a Saturday night than opening a favorite bottle of Chianti and memorizing the Excel keyboard shortcuts. More resourceful Alpha Weasels spend their weekends redrafting the company organizational charts, placing themselves in positions of power should they discover any gray area in the chain of command. They often assume that everyone else is working on the weekend too, calling coworkers on their cells on Saturday night to check the status of the i-Centrics account.

Nevertheless, Alpha Weasels do let their hair down occasionally. Sometimes during happy hour they've been known to discuss very personal details about themselves, like their feelings on departmental accountability issues or the sadness they felt when the company Web team phased out the interactive client outreach quiz.

The Rounder-Upper

Alpha Weasels function in an unofficial capacity as the company **Rounder-Uppers**. Before any given meeting, they walk down the aisles of the office saying "Come on, guys, quit what you're doing. The meeting is at three. Let's get moving." Some emphasize a sense of urgency with a clap or two of their hands. Others supplement a verbal reminder with e-mails and Post-it notes. By assuming the role of Rounder-Upper, Alpha Weasels indirectly acquire dominance over their coworkers.

The Company Meeting

Since the ultimate goal of all Alpha Weasels is to move up the corporate ladder, the company meeting is very important to furthering their ambitions. Refusing to sit back and passively wait for others to initiate meetings, Alpha Weasels organize dozens of meetings in any given workweek. Using meticulously designed visual aids created in PowerPoint and exhaustively detailed handouts, Alpha Weasels are experts at conducting meetings on an array of topics, such as:

▶ Should files be named using upper- or lowercase letters?
▶ Is it appropriate to use smiley faces or wingdings when communicating with clients?
▶ Should that window by Mary's desk *ever* be opened after November?
▶ Should employees really be listening to music while at work?
▶ Is calling me anally retentive respectful or acceptable, *under ANY circumstance*?

When not running a meeting, Alpha Weasels refuse to play second fiddle and ensure that they're the center of attention by sitting next to the person in

PLUG (Idio Rank: 3.1)

Everyone is familiar with the cranky, condescending tech guy (the Linux) who sullenly refuses to speak in layman's terms when discussing your computer. His attitude is as thick as the Medieval Club plate-mail armor he has at home. Plug, on the other hand, defies the negative tech person stereotypes with his boredom-induced warmth and good cheer. Since his job entails troubleshooting tech issues, he's often allotted extra free time when no one is having specific problems with their computers. Plug likes to stare over your shoulder and make sure you're utilizing your programs to their full capacity. He takes the extra time to show you all the keyboard shortcuts and tricks, especially when you're running late for a meeting. When crunch time rolls around for a project, Plug never gets his assignments completed because he's too concerned with showing others how things "should" work. Plug is also mesmerized by anything attached to a cord and often sidles up next to coworkers who have access to high-tech scanners, cameras, and hardware, admiring the equipment like a kid in a candy store. If you're using new software that Plug hasn't mastered himself, he'll be your companion until the bitter end. To be fair, Plug does spend some time at his own desk, usually downloading spywear or making electronic music based on mathematical algorithms.

charge. This provides them with opportunities to nod approvingly and to interject with their own comments. It also endows them with **Proximity Clout**, since sitting next to an authority figure psychologically implies dominance. Alpha Weasels also understand the importance of getting in the last word and state enthusiastically: "Well, guys, let's get the ball rolling!" should they luck into a pregnant pause at the close of a meeting.

The Healing Powers of Popcorn

Many Alpha Weasels are initially blind to the hostility they create around them, but with time the tension they generate becomes too much to ignore. Alpha Weasels who fear that they're sabotaging themselves with their own overzealousness will inevitably begin to worry that severed office relations could reflect poorly on their performance reviews.

Knowing that nothing makes people happier than free food, some begin bringing cookies to meetings or make microwave popcorn to show that work can be fun. Others position Beanie Babies on top of their monitors to illustrate that they have big hearts after all.

Another common tactic employed by Alpha Weasels to alleviate work tension is to try to secure allies by organizing company outings such as picnics, bowling night, and karaoke Thursdays. More desperate Alpha Weasels may even attempt to integrate themselves into company cliques by stopping by a key member's cube to ask, "So where's the gang going for lunch today?" When successful at securing an invite, they do their best to impress their new "friends" by saying things like, "I *love* the Dead. You know, I used to be a partier in college." Despite their efforts, Alpha Weasels are often given secret nicknames by their coworkers like Captain Ritalin, Speedy, or simply Shithead.

It should be noted that two Alpha Weasels cannot peacefully coexist in any one office, given their overly competitive natures. Although there are two cheeks to kiss on any given boss's ass, the weaker contender will ultimately tire of getting sloppy seconds.

 CHECK-MATES (Idio Rank: 5.4)

Check-Mates are office buddies who corner you into being their friends. *Are you going out for lunch today? Want to grab a drink tonight after work? Why aren't you signed onto Instant Messenger anymore? Mind if I swing by your cube to talk about my boyfriend/girlfriend, who is giving me mixed signals about whether or not he/she really likes me ever since we slept together?* Sound familiar? To beat this overbearing coworker at his own game, we recommend outbuddying him. Here are some suggestions:

1. Save his picture as your desktop wallpaper.
2. Staple your finger and ask if he wants to be blood brothers.
3. Offer to give him a piggyback ride to the four o'clock meeting.
4. Leave a copy of *Fatal Attraction* and a drawing of a dead bunny on his desk.
5. Offer to build a fort with him using the sofa cushions from the reception area.

6 | The Lifer

IN BRIEF: Intelligent but socially inept employees who lack the motivation to look for another job in this lifetime

POPULATION SIZE: Common

GENDER: Male or female

HABITAT: Basement apartments, at home with the folks

HOBBIES: Watching strays in the alley, sometimes feeding strays in the alley

FAVORITE BOOKS: *Crime and Punishment*, *Essential Pieces for the Eastern European Postage Stamp Connoisseur*

SCREEN SAVER: An iconic philosopher, a Teletubby

IDIO RANK: 6.5

Overview

If you work in a large corporate setting for a time-established employer, chances are you know a Lifer. The Lifer is an unambitious lower-level employee who has been with the company since the dawn of man. When inquiries are made into the actual start date of a Lifer, senior staffers tend to scratch their heads before asking in resignation, "Hasn't he *always* been here?"

Note: Though it's not as accurate as carbon dating, one can generally estimate a start date by noting the degree to which the ink has faded on the Lifer's stapler label.

As counterintuitive as it may seem, Lifers are bitter about their vocational fate and rarely enjoy working for the institutions for which they're employed. Whereas occupational allegiance generally arises from satisfaction with what one does for a living, the Lifer's commitment to the company comes by default for the following reasons:

- Deviating from their routines makes them panic or sweat.
- They're making just enough to pay rent and buy two comic books a week.
- Their current job provides them with free pencils.
- They have too many MP3s on their hard drive to leave.
- They have a genetic predisposition to heavy breathing, which frightens would-be employers.

It should be noted that some Lifers are conspiracy buffs and fear that the government agents who have been following them will finally make their move should they attempt to find work elsewhere.

Spotting a Lifer

Every Idio Type has a distinguishing characteristic, and when it comes to the Lifer, this characteristic is dandruff. Whether or not they are cognizant of the plaster-sized chips on their shoulders is unclear, but needless to say, everyone else Lifers come in contact with is sure to notice. In general, Lifers tend to be very unkempt, often wearing the same outdated work duds day after day. On the rare occasion they purchase new outfits, Lifers prefer thrift shops and stores that specialize in drawstrings, like the Comfort Zone.

Though the particulars of their aroma change with age, Lifers are also easily identified by the way they smell. Lifers who are in their thirties opt for a powdery, deodorant-and-sweat theme. As they transition into their forties, it begins to ripen into a moldy aroma, often with a hint of mothballs. And when it comes to Lifers who are fifty or older, one should expect a more complex smell that blends powder, sweat, and mothballs with subtle hints of pee, or sometimes vinegar.

Lifers tend to carry brown paper bags that contain their lunches. They are loners at heart and packing a lunch keeps them from having to bend to the peer pressure of going to the cafeteria or food court with their coworkers. Since they tend to be avid collectors, packing a lunch also helps them save a few bucks to spend on their music, stamp, or child pornography collections. Many Lifers have neurotic tics and quirks. Atonal humming, nail biting, and an insistence upon using only number 3 pencils are some common examples.

The Lifer Wisdom

Lifers play an important role in the office because they acquire unconventional wisdom that leads coworkers to seek them out for advice. Where the typical longtime employee can go into great detail about work-related particulars of the company, the Lifer's knowledge is much more intimate. The Lifer would know, for instance, that Veronica keeps a flask of bourbon in her top drawer and she once slept with the guy who checks the ink levels on the copy machine.

Lifers are too misanthropic to really be gossipers, but when pressed they love to reveal the salaries of everyone in their department. When the mood strikes them, Lifers can become great storytellers, passing on the oral tradition of the company from one generation to the next. Sometimes they embellish, turning a simple piece of office lore about a former employee who was fired into a nuanced cautionary tale.

Home Away from Home

Like old couples who fart in front of one another because they've been together so long, Lifers inevitably become too comfortable at work. Over time, their sense of decorum becomes diluted. A Lifer, for instance, would have no qualm asking a colleague to finish collating for him since "his hemorrhoids are flaring up."

Many Lifers begin to think of the office as their home away from home. They take their belts and shoes off at their desks, oblivious to the frustration they may be causing the person in the next cube over as they smack their lips eating Cool Ranch Doritos. Some Lifers even begin to treat their coworkers like roommates, leaving Post-its on their computer monitors to voice concerns about not replacing paper in the copy machine. They often decorate their cubes with plants, calendars, and action figures and stock the refrigerator with condiments and Tupperware.

Commonly, Lifers become paranoid about food theft, given that fishy incident with the missing Mountain Dew. They keep a watchful eye on whoever enters the kitchen and write their names on the mayonnaise and ketchup containers. One should be sure to dispose of Chinese leftovers, since failing to maintain the fridge is a sure way to become the object of a Lifer's discontent. Disgruntled Lifers have been known to ambush unsuspecting coworkers with flailing arms. They're sometimes unaware of their own strength.

Nevertheless, Lifers are a vital part of any given office environment, bringing continuity to the workplaces they inhabit by bridging generations of employees, past and present, together.

7 | Hall Monitors

IN BRIEF: The lovable guy in the office whose lack of diligence is overlooked because he's so darn nice

POPULATION SIZE: Moderately common

GENDER: Male

HABITAT: Wandering the halls and cubicle aisles (especially in Sales)

HOBBIES: Organizing fantasy sports leagues and Oscar pools

POPULAR NICKNAMES: Hoss, the Mikester, Craigarino, Jim Dawg

SCREEN SAVER: Sports team logos

IDIO RANK: 2.8

Overview

Similar to the way *Saturday Night Live* must always have an endearing fat guy to round out the cast, every office has a Hall Monitor. When it comes to anything outside the realm of television, sports, or pop culture, Hall Monitors are borderline retarded, but they're so agreeable and good-natured that they appeal to everyone nonetheless.

Hall Monitors are always lighthearted and optimistic, bringing good cheer to everyone around them. In lieu of having witty senses of humor, they simply shower their coworkers with fun phrases recycled from television, like "Waassuuup?" or "Did you finizzle your repizzle?"

Older Hall Monitors who have become out of touch may embarrass themselves by blurting out dated pop culturisms like "Hey, Maggie, where's the beef?" Others delight their coworkers by "doing the stairs," a hilarious trick that involves buckling one's knees and pretending to descend an imaginary stairway.

Taking a Hit for the Team

Beyond simply bringing levity and cheer to the office, the Hall Monitor plays an important role as the object of the office clown's jokes. Though most offices have their own share of social outcasts who are more obvious targets, making socially challenged coworkers the brunt of your jokes can foster resentment and is generally considered to be bad office politics. Since Hall Monitors are mild tempered, they're the perfect target for office teasing. In fact, they tend to enjoy the attention. After the chuckles subside they simply shake their head and offer a falsetto rebuttal of "You people are *crazy*" or, in some less politically correct offices, "At least I'm not gay!"

Coming Through in the Clutch

Though Hall Monitors are only sporadically hardworking, coworkers never question their competence because they're so doggone likable. When they apply themselves they're quite good at what they do, but most Hall Monitors prefer spending their time socializing and giving high fives. In fact, 90 percent of their workday involves meandering through the aisles laughing good-naturedly at their coworkers' jokes. Bosses tend to turn a blind eye to their lighthearted ways, confident that when the time comes, Hall Monitors know how to buckle down. Hall Monitors are universally praised for their ability to come through in the clutch, even though they rarely know what the phrase actually means.

Image Is Everything

Since their endearing personalities are their largest asset, Hall Monitors do everything they can to help perpetuate their image. When it comes to winning over female coworkers, placing a picture of their wife or girlfriend on their desk never fails to impress. It's a simple gesture that suggests a sweetness and harmlessness that's uncommon these days. More importantly, Hall Monitors are always sensitive of women's feelings and would never stare at a coworker's boobs unless she's too preoccupied to notice. When it comes to the men of the office, Hall Monitors are always generous and fair with their delivery of pats to the back.

The Hall Monitor's Secret Power

As most will attest, recognition at work is rarely a result of one's diligence or merit. Instead, your success and/or failure rates are in direct proportion to how popular you are. Coworkers who are cognizant of this will not be surprised to discover that becoming part of the Hall Monitor's inner circle guarantees upward mobility. Should you achieve this coveted position, the boss will immediately assume you're cool and fun; with time, your promotion is ensured. Inversely, those who are out of favor with the Hall Monitor should consider their days limited. Ironically, Hall Monitors should never communicate a desire for promotion themselves since being carefree and noncompetitive is integral to their own success.

 MILKERS (Idio Rank: 7.1)

The Milker is a passive-aggressive coworker who wants you to do all of his work for him. Milkers are easily identified in the office given their tendency to say, "Do you mind showing me how to fill out this report?" "Do you mind discussing my policy frustrations with him for me?" and "Do you mind grabbing me a salad from Cosí?"

Sometimes being candid at work can be uncomfortable, but standing up for yourself when dealing with a Milker is important. A diplomatic rebuttal like "Do you mind getting out of my face before I invoke the Lord of the soulless to feast on the blood of children at the altar of your impending doom?" will generally help to alleviate any problems you have with a Milker and ensure that the least amount of productivity is lost.

8 | Straightshooters

IN BRIEF: An earnest-talking, micromanaging, office-jargon aficionado who has no hands-on knowledge of company procedures or logistics

POPULATION SIZE: Common

GENDER: Male or female

HABITAT: McMansions in treeless housing developments

HOBBIES: Reading our nation's paper, *USA Today*, collecting metal band wristwatches

SCREEN SAVER: None

IDIO RANK: 6.1

Overview

Working with a Straightshooter is as fundamental to the modern-day office experience as fluorescent lighting, wall-to-wall carpet, and burned coffee. Straightshooters rarely take their duties very seriously, but it's important to them to appear diligent in order to gain acceptance and power within the office hierarchy. Straightshooters know that the higher they move up the corporate ladder, the less work they'll have to do. They become well versed in corporate jargon to cloak their ineptitude and to ensure that their stock options remain securely intact.

Talking the Talk

Straightshooters get their name from their tendency to *appear* like they are speaking frankly in situations that would generally call for diplomacy or evasive talk. Under close scrutiny, it becomes obvious that Straightshooters rarely show candor and instead employ distraction and office jargon to their advantage. In most situations, Straightshooters follow four simple conversational rules when interacting with coworkers:

1. State up front that you are being honest or candid.
2. Using strong eye contact, address the individual you're talking to by name and/or with a friendly touch to the shoulder.
3. Incorporate at least two instances of office jargon into your exposition.
4. Finally, ask the individual about his family/weekend/significant other to alleviate tension.

EXAMPLE

Addressing the boss:
Well, Mike, let me be honest with you, I'll front-burner that, but we have so much on our plates right now, it's going to take some strategizing. But don't you worry; we're prepared to tighten our belts. Hey, how's your wife?

Addressing a subordinate:
I'm not going to beat around the bush, Mary. We need to be in a firefighting mode if we want to synergize our bottom line this quarter. I just wanted to touch base about this. By the way, how'd your cousin's surgery go?

Some Straightshooters deploy a fifth "exit step" by saying "thanks, big guy" or "you the man." Older Straightshooters often prefer the **exit wink**.

When talking to coworkers, Straightshooters commonly use acronyms such as DRI (Directly Responsible Individual) and WWS (win-win situation) to confuse their peers into believing that they know what they're talking about.

I'll front-burner that—I'll get around to that as soon as I get the high score on this 3-D Tetris game I downloaded.

Think outside the box—Be imaginative; for example, pretend your cubicle isn't a creativity-stifling sarcophagus.

We're in firefighting mode—We fucked up royally.

Tighten our belts—Everybody will be working longer and harder with no additional pay while I'm at Hooters.

Pencil me in—I have every intention of finding an excuse to avoid this commitment.

What's on your plate?—1. Why aren't you working? 2. I feel the need to reestablish my authority over you.

Bustin' your chops—I just made an inappropriate comment and now want to pretend it never happened.

Takin' the high road—I turned the other cheek, you know, just like Jesus would.

We're transitioning you—You'll be responsible for additional petty and degrading tasks. And no, you are not getting a raise.

Synergize—Meaning unknown.

OTHER FAVORITE STRAIGHTSHOOTER PLATITUDES

Touch base	Team player
Ducks in a row	Keep it in the end zone
Proactive	Push back
Raising the bar	Drop the ball
Reprioritize	Blamestorming

The Go-Getter Style

Male Straightshooters are easily spotted since they tend to carry briefcases and/or attaché cases and wear paisley ties, vests, pleated pants, and, sometimes, suspenders. They're also fond of their high school rings and wear them for life. Female Straightshooters love the fashion of the eighties and sometimes wonder why Nancy Reagan hasn't started her own clothing line. Both genders carry themselves with abnormally good posture and practice their eye contact skills with their spouses, children, pets, and stuffed animals.

Straightshooters who are still moving up the company ladder make it a point to befriend the company bigwigs, thus gaining power by association. Overly transparent brownnosing by Straightshooters can at times cause conflict for them. Should tension arise, they often begin carrying squeeze balls to appear more fun.

The Early Bird Flies Beneath the Radar

Understanding the power of *the early arrival*, Straightshooters are always among the first to make an appearance in the morning. They know that arriving early is an easy way to seem on top of things. Besides, slipping out the back door at three o'clock will generally go unnoticed and is much more socially acceptable than arriving late. Many Straightshooters prefer sales jobs or positions that require travel so they can claim they're "out in the field" if questioned about their absence. "Out in the field" of course being code for enjoying margaritas and poppers at Applebee's on the company plastic.

Making the Rounds

To announce their presence in the morning, Straightshooters enter the building talking jovially on their cell phones. *Hi, Chuck, I'm going to take the high road and touch base with the Motorola rep today.* As they enter, they immediately turn on any lights dimmed by their morning-weary coworkers to signal that the day has officially begun. Anyone who doesn't prefer a bright office is either inept, a Communist, or on drugs.

Understanding that eating breakfast on your feet makes you look like a go-getter, Straightshooters travel from cubicle to cubicle with a muffin and coffee to check the status of any projects in the works. Since Straightshooters universally wear Chaps, English Leather, or Old Spice cologne (females prefer Liz Claiborne products), coworkers who familiarize themselves with these scents will be able to detect the approach of a Straightshooter and avoid being caught off guard by an unexpected visit.

The Company Meeting

Straightshooters are enviably gifted public speakers. They can improvise on a wide array of topics during company meetings, such as team player ethics, optimization, the nitty-gritty, and keeping your eyes on the bottom line. All Straightshooters know that making a speech at the onset of a meeting grants them the option to excuse themselves "to take an important call."

Beyond the Workplace

Outside the office, Straightshooters often find that sports metaphors are more versatile than office-specific rhetoric. *I thought Mike was going to drop the ball on this one, Pete, but he really seems to be keeping his marriage in the end zone.* Nevertheless, Straightshooters regularly confound their friends and families by using rhetoric that is awkward and inappropriate outside a work environment. To avoid arguing at the dinner table in front of the kids, for instance, Straightshooters infuriate their partners by saying "Can we talk about this offline?"

 THE GIGGLER (Idio Rank: 6.3)

It's 10 A.M. and your coffee has just kicked in. The office has finally become quiet, save the gentle hum of the flickering overhead light in the corner. The morning bustle has subsided and all is still. Suddenly you hear it, a high-pitched, breathy *tee, hee, hee, heee, chorkle, weee!* It's the Giggler. No one is quite sure what he's laughing at, but some worry that he may have some type of "special" problem. Some hypothesize that he's discovered the Warn button on Instant Messenger and this is the source of his joy. Others think it may have something to do with the Cosby sweater Stan is wearing. Thankfully, breaks are guaranteed from the revelry throughout the day as the Giggler is prone to excessive naps. Stealing one of his Homey figurines when he gets up to go to the bathroom will generally be a big enough buzz kill to subdue his giggles for a few hours.

CATSCAN* Number 1

Want to escape a dreary life among the cubes? Dennis M. Hope, CEO and president of the Galactic Government and the Lunar Embassy, proves that clever entrepreneurship can pave the way to success.

A former unemployed ventriloquist, Hope founded the Lunar Embassy, a company that claims to be "the leaders in extraterrestrial real estate and the ONLY company in the world to be recognized to possess a legal basis for selling and registering extraterrestrial properties." In other words, he claims to own the moon. Not to mention all the other planets (and *their* moons) in our solar system, with the exception of Earth, of course.

In 1980, Hope wrote to the United Nations after finding a loophole in the International Outer Space Treaty that only prohibits *governments* and *businesses* from claiming ownership of extraterrestrial bodies. The treaty says nothing about *private individuals* owning and profiting from them. The Moon Treaty, which was drafted in 1979, would have rectified this problem, but most nations (including the United States) have yet to sign it. Since no one has officially contested his claims, Hope insists he is the rightful owner of the moon, Mars, and Jupiter.

The good news is that for just $19.99 you, too, can own a moon plot. (Interplanetary tax comes to about a buck fifty.) All moon plots offer "prime views" of Earth. Hope currently lives in Gardnerville, Nevada, and has never visited the moon, Mars, or any of Jupiter's moons himself.

He has, however, set up a Declaration of Galactic Independence, which states (in part):

> "We, the Human Beings of the planet Earth who are the heirs, gentry, and citizens of the Galactic Government, do hereby declare our intention to break the gravitational and political bounds that keep us on Earth so that we might venture forth to find a new combined destiny of Life, Liberty, and the pursuit of Happiness."

Mars even has its own constitution and Bill of Rights. An amazingly thorough businessman, Hope has even drafted laws to answer land ownership questions should the red planet prove to be inhabited:

· · · **36** · · ·

The Galactic flag

"If such life exists (sentient or not) and it is capable of letting you know by means of any form of communications (language, gestures, etc.) that we (and you) are not welcome on its property, unfortunately, then, we have all lost all our rights altogether."

Unfortunately, if you're interested in buying a plot of land on one of Mars's moons, you'll have to wait. They are not up for sale quite yet.

So this all raises the question, "Who's buying this property anyway?" Hope cannot reveal the names of buyers since confidentiality is guaranteed with each purchase, but he claims that two former U.S. presidents as well as more than 250 "well-known celebrities" own extraterrestrial property.

Hope has made millions (approximately $6.5 million) and, as of last count, sold 2,000,047 plots. And though he claims that people commonly "buy them as gifts for their loved ones," we personally don't recommend buying them as anniversary presents or Valentine's Day gifts. Unless your significant other is really into *Star Trek*.

Nevertheless, you can buy a plot for your dream home on the moon today at www.lunarembassy.com.

The Gag Order
(The Family and the Conversationally Challenged)

No one has a "normal" family. In one way or another, even the most conventional-seeming family is eccentric. Everyone has a few bizarre family members. The overly nurturing brother who tells you not to sit too close to the TV. The aunt who collects nautical-themed thimbles. The grandmother who enjoys showing off her Utah travel brochures. The cousin who's in a Poison tribute band.

Paradoxically, people simultaneously tend to feel comfortable and on edge when with their families. Odd behavior is a given when you're surrounded by the ones you're tied to by blood. When with their families, people say and do things they'd never even consider saying or doing at work or among friends.

Some people, on the other hand, don't need the catalyst of family to provoke conversational strangeness. People who overutilize sports metaphors. WASPs who try to talk "street" when they're around blacks. Corny people who insist upon saying "anywho." People who make a habit of saying "I'm not religious, but I'm spiritual." These people are neurotic all on their own.

The following section unveils our research into family-based Idio Types and Idio Types that have an unconventional way of communicating. More often than not, the two are intertwined.

 This image indicates that more thorough research on this particular Idio Type is pending.

9 | Granny Dickens

IN BRIEF: Overly candid letter writers who reveal personal and/
   or demoralizing information in their uncensored diatribes
POPULATION SIZE: Moderately common
GENDER: Female
HABITAT: The ointment aisle at Piggly Wiggly
HOBBIES: Clipping coupons, trying to figure out the e-mail
IDIO RANK: 5.7

Overview

Every family has its own letter writer, usually an aunt or grandmother who keeps everyone up-to-date on the details of the family in exhaustively thorough quarterly newsletters. Did Jeremy get accepted at UCLA? Was it a snowy winter in Boston? Who's expecting a baby? All of these questions are answered in painstaking detail by the family letter writer.

A less common but ever more thorough breed of letter writer is the Idio Type known as the Granny Dickens. Granny Dickenses are notoriously tactless chroniclers who keep the family abreast on much more intimate topics: Has Stanley been having regular bowel movements? Is Jason still wearing black torn clothing like a drug addict? Will Jim's wandering eye affect his marriage *this* year?

With the dawn of e-mail, many Granny Dickenses delight in the larger audience they can reach with their letters. Now with a click of a button, they can send useful information about bacterial infections, canker sores, and stool softeners to everyone in their address book.

A Typical Letter by a Granny Dickens

Hello Everyone:

Sorry it has been so long, loves. You all know how time flies. Stanley and I made it through another year and many trials and tribulations. I thought I'd catch everybody up on all the news. We know the holidays are *BUSY,* but hope you all can make the time to stop by. We have a new humidifier and our home doesn't feel dry like it used to. Stanley just finished putting up the Christmas tree. He hates when I say it, but his hemorrhoids are still bothering him plenty. On a positive note, our new humidifier seems to help his psoriasis.

As you all know, our granddaughter Mary started high school this year, down at Midlothian. Her mother insists on working still, so we've been looking after her. Mary was doing some better in Math and got moved into the class for regular students. Unfortunately, she may need to return to the class for slower children. She got a D last quarter. I told her mother she wasn't ready for the regular class but she never listens. Nevertheless, Mary seems to have exited her awkward stage and has really been coming into her own. Her complexion (which as you all know was b-a-d) has cleared up. She has really gotten big up top, too. Seems like that happened overnight! She's been talking on the phone more now, I presume to boys. She needs to stand up straight and work on her posture. No sense in hiding what you got. She looks pretty and we are proud of her.

I finally got the yard cleaned up after that big storm we had in November. Boy was that a lot of work. You wouldn't believe how many sticks were down. Ms. Difalco next door still hasn't cleaned up her mess. She's as lazy as a tick, and I just know she thinks I raked leaves into her ditch. I certainly did not. They get pushed down there sometimes by the rain. She's always so worrisome but I just keep praying.

I finally got my teeth fixed. I have two new molars to replace the stumps I had before. You can barely tell they're not real. And good news, I started Stanley and myself on a fiber-enriched diet that seems to be making us much more regular. As you all know we both have had problems with having a regular BM. (ESPECIALLY Stanley!) If you haven't tried it already, Uncle Sam cereal is very nutritious. Plus it's a natural laxative. Says so right on the box. Eating lots of asparagus seems to be helping too. Keeping Stanley away from candy and potato chips is a full-time job. It sure is.

Another year without a cavity though. Does everyone know about tongue brushing? I'd never even thought to do it, but Dr. Chovev says that the film builds up on your tongue and can cause bad breath (someone should tell Aunt Claire). Sure enough, I dragged some floss across my tongue and there was LOTS of residue there. Bet you have some too (it will look milky white). I think the humidifier helps because dry air can cause film to build up too I bet.

Lord almighty, I nearly forgot to mention, Mike and Mary are separated. Nobody knows why, but I've got my suspicions (you know I don't like to gossip). I ran into them together at Best Buy a month ago and they just seemed nervous, I could tell something was going on. He was unemployed for the longest time but works down at Big Lots now. That Jenkins girl from down the road works there too.

The good news is we have a new precious addition to the family. A new cat! We call her Mandrell after Barbara (well at least I do, I can't repeat what Stanley calls her, ha!). She's a joy. Her fur is very puffy and elegant, like a show cat. We bought her one of those "toilet attachments" that go on top of the commode. What will they think of next?! Now if she would just learn to flush! She likes the humidifier too because it helps her dandruff.

I'm going to make a better effort to see Aunt Ethel more often since nobody else in the family takes the time. She likes to go to Lila's Steakhouse. They have a magnificent buffet with beef macaroni and cheese and soft ice cream. Stanley always wants to eat too much there and makes himself sick. I know now to bring his medicine to the restaurant in my purse. We both need to get back to the gastro-intestinal doctor, not to mention the chiropractor.

Granny Dickens

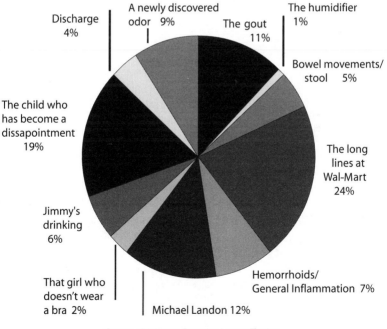

Granny Dickens: Popular Letter Topics

RING WORMS (Idio Rank: 7.4)

Ring Worms are people who are addicted to talking on their cell phones. When ordering a cappuccino at a café, they multitask by making a call while they order. They bring their phones out on dates and phone friends to tell them how things are going right after the entrées arrive. They stare at their phones and giggle, messaging friends while you're trying to talk to them. When you tell Ring Worms that they're being rude, they uniformly get indignant and exclaim, "Lighten up, I need to use all my free minutes." Extremely obnoxious Ring Worms are sometimes called **Cellholes**.

FLAIRHEADS (Idio Rank: 6.5)

FlairHeads are airheaded women who flirt with men because they have nothing else to say. They've always been physically desirable and therefore never felt the need to develop a personality of their own. Flirting and looking good have always gotten them everything they wanted. When the conversation gets too cerebral, they change the subject by complimenting your accent or by saying they like the sexy way your lips shake when you get excited about that political stuff.

FlairHeads regularly utter unintentionally provocative statements like "Wow, you look hot in that color. *I'd* do you." They're confounded that anyone could interpret this as a come-on. To them, harmless compliments like this simply keep the conversation from getting all heavy and boring. Men who marry FlairHeads are often cornered by well-meaning friends who say, "Dude, don't get mad, but I think your wife is coming on to me." Most shrug the accusations off, knowing that their lover is just a little deficient in the conversation department.

An easy way to ascertain if a woman is a FlairHead is by asking her what type of music she likes. If she responds by saying "I like all kinds of music" or "I love reggae," she's probably a FlairHead. It's a mystery, but all FlairHeads uniformly reply with one of these two responses.

10 | Zingers

IN BRIEF: People who constantly yell out punch lines from movies, commercials, and television

POPULATION SIZE: Common

GENDER: Male or female

HABITAT: "Chillin', like Bob Dylan" in movie theaters and in front of the TV

HOBBIES: Practicing Tony Soprano, Christopher Walken, Barbara Walters impersonations

IDIO RANK: 4.8

Overview

In the pop-culture-saturated times that we live in, most of our cherished cultural expressions come from television, the movies, and commercials. Everyone is familiar with the famous *Star Wars* quote "May the force be with you" and the *Star Trek* catchphrase "Damnit, Jim, I'm a doctor." Just hearing a favorite line from a movie or TV show can bring the joy of recognition. When used appropriately, quoting a memorable line can even win you a few laughs at work, at church, at a club, or on that important date.

A common Idio Type known as the Zinger shapes his/her entire personality around quoting movies and TV. Having no sense of humor of their own, Zingers quote knowingly and frequently from a wide array of comedies, dramas, *SNL* skits, and beer commercials. They know that if Austin Powers can sell a million tickets saying "Yeeaa Babeey," they sure as heck can secure that important work account by saying it. And if Mike Myers can do fifteen sequels, why not recycle his gleeful catchphrase over and over again too?

The Classic Zinger Hall of Fame

Most overused
"I'll be back."—*The Terminator*
Most versatile
"You can't HANDLE the truth."—*A Few Good Men*
Most commonly whispered to a coworker in a tense meeting
"I love the smell of napalm in the morning."—*Apocalypse Now*
Most homophobic
"You sure got a purty mouth."—*Deliverance*
Most commonly employed with a bad impersonation
"I'm gonna make him an offer he can't refuse."—*The Godfather*
Most commonly used by people with hair plugs
"If I'm not back in five minutes . . . just wait longer."—*Ace Ventura*
Most interchangeable
"You looking at me?"/"Do I amuse you?"—*Taxi Driver* and *GoodFellas*
Most able to stand the test of time
"Looks like I picked the wrong week to stop sniffing glue."
—*Airplane*
Most trite
"This is the beginning of a beautiful friendship."—*Casablanca*
Most annoying
"Show me the money."—*Jerry Maguire*
Least likely to make a comeback
"He slimed me."—*Ghostbusters*
Most appropriate when talking about a Zinger's use of quotes
"It's social. Demented and sad, but social."—*The Breakfast Club*

Common Zinger Misconception

The Zinger's appreciation for film is generally no greater than that of the typical moviegoer. Though some Zingers are movie buffs, most quote lines out of necessity. They simply don't have anything of their own to say. Most Zingers fail to realize that their constant referencing of pop culture is an obvious crutch.

Granted, when meeting someone whose Friendster profile states "looking for someone with a sense of humor," having some clever movie lines to quote can come in handy. Nevertheless, should their date not recognize a film reference, it can blow up in a Zinger's face. Especially with those who push the boundaries with more risky lines like "I ate his liver with some fava beans and a nice Chianti."

Remember This Line?

All Zingers have fine-tuned the art of recall. They know that anyone can remember television lines like "for me to poop on" or "I love it when a plan comes together." These phrases have been broadcast so many times that they're burned into the public consciousness. Zingers know that integrating overused TV lines into conversation is for novices and are sure to have dozens of more esoteric phrases at their disposal.

Remembering fleeting lines from movies is a more challenging task, especially since most Zingers also try to do impressions of the actors who originally utter them. Zingers know that quoting properly is hard work and practice their lines until they're perfected. Those who are bad at impressions simply develop their own "wacky voice," a more nasal or high-pitched version of their natural speaking voice.

Zinger Faux Pas

Since Zingers are very quick on the draw, many bring trouble for themselves by using movie quotes inappropriately. For instance, should the company CEO enter the boardroom to update the staff, utilizing the popular Jack Nicholson line "Heeere's Johnny" probably isn't the best idea. Should a Zinger find himself at an AA meeting, the line from *Animal House* "My advice to you is to start drinking heavily" should probably be avoided in response to a group member's earnest testimony. And though the line from *Raising Arizona* "Her womb was a rocky place where my seed could find no purchase" is undeniably memorable, friends may find it an insensitive way to describe personal details about your wife. It probably goes without saying, but "Here's looking at you kid" is never a good line to use at a singles bar.

The Mirimax

High-profile films such as *Die Hard*, *American Pie*, and *Meet the Parents* have provided a wealth of material for a multitude of Zingers nationwide. Nevertheless, some Zingers are more discriminating than others and wouldn't be caught dead shooting off an obvious quote like "Dude, where's my car?"

Mirimaxes are the ultimate zinger connoisseurs. They prefer quoting more highbrow phrases like *Dr. Strangelove*'s "Gentlemen, you can't fight in here. This is the War Room." *Donnie Darko*, *Soylent Green*, *Cabin Boy*, *Repo Man*, *Blue Velvet*, and *American Movie* are the preferred source material for Mirimaxes. They enjoy referencing mainstream biggies as well, but choose the forgotten zingers like *Airplane*'s "Do you like movies about gladiators?" in favor of the overused "Don't call me Shirley" line.

The Mirimax's Top Ten Movie Quotes

10. "Bring out your dead."—*Monty Python and the Holy Grail*
9. "Excuse me while I whip this out."—*Blazing Saddles*
8. "They're nihilists, Donny, nothing to be afraid of."—*The Big Lebowski*
7. "That's what I like about these high school girls, I keep getting older, they stay the same age."—*Dazed and Confused*
6. "You make it with some of these chicks, and they think you gotta dance with them."—*Saturday Night Fever*
5. "I haven't been fucked like that since grade school."—*Fight Club*
4. "Now ain't that a shame when folks be throwing away a perfectly good white boy like that."—*Better Off Dead*
3. "If things go right I might be showing her my O-face. You know: Oh! Oh!"—*Office Space*
2. "We have both kinds of music. Country and western."—*The Blues Brothers*
1. "These ones go up to eleven."—*Spinal Tap*

Other Types of Zingers

GROENERS

Named for the *Simpsons* creator Matt Groening, Groeners are obsessed with the uber-popular Fox cartoon family. Groeners rarely blurt out individual lines from the show. After all, any fan of the *Simpsons* can sprinkle conversation with a well-placed "d'oh" or a reference to Duff beer. Groeners prefer recapping entire monologues. Plus, they're always *Simpsons* trivia experts and can tell you that Captain McAllister said "Arrr, I hate the sea and everything in it" in episode thirty-two, season five. All Groeners get a little defensive should you claim to like Bart more than Homer, who is obviously the superior character.

JUMPING BEANS (Idio Rank: 6.1)

Jumping Beans are people who unexpectedly jump into a Spanish accent midsentence when pronouncing the word "Latino," only to finish their statement in accent-free English. Though Jumping Beans were at one time Latino newscasters exclusively, people of any race or occupation can now be Jumping Beans. In fact, the trend today is increasingly popular with a diverse group of people ranging from whites to blacks, from accountants to lawyers. In the past, many Jumping Beans were erroneously diagnosed with multiple personality disorder, given the seamless way they jumped in and out of a Spanish accent without batting an eye. Today, pronouncing the word "Latino" with an accent is accepted as being semantically sensitive and even a progressive way to give Latinos a shout-out. Curiously, Jumping Beans rarely pronounce the words "Japanese," "German," "Southern," or "Israeli" with their respective accents. Luckily, the Columbia School of Journalism has a new class called "From Argentinean to Zimbabwean: Sensitive Heritage Pronunciation for Aspiring News Anchors and Weathermen."

CRYSTAL MEGS

Crystal Megs quote cliché relationship questions posed by the popular Billy Crystal–Meg Ryan movie *When Harry Met Sally.* . . . "Doesn't it feel great just to sit with someone and not talk?" "Can men and women just be friends?" and "Do women ever fake it?" are key questions that need to be pondered in life. Discussing the common topics brought up in *When Harry Met Sally* . . . really comes in handy when discussing relationships on gals' night or as an icebreaker when getting more serious with someone special. Crystal Megs understand that all you really need to know about love was covered by this classic date film.

THE OBSCURO

Obscuros regularly reference *21 Jump Street*, *Deep Star Six*, and *Amityville Dollhouse*. They use quotes awkwardly, attempting to transform a line like *Newhart*'s "Say hello to Darryl, his brother Darryl, and his other brother Darryl" into a lewd comment. Obscuros also fail to realize the expiration date has passed on quotes like "Danger, Will Robinson" and are surprised when met with raised eyebrows as they attempt to integrate them into conversation. Needless to say, the Obscuro has few friends.

THE TOTAL RECALL

Total Recalls are Arnold Schwarzenegger–quoting liberals who just don't feel right saying "It's not a tumah" anymore, now that Arnold is the governor of California. They keep their fingers crossed that Tim Robbins or Moby will begin doing action movies that will provide them with some worthy substitutions.

 **Flourettes and Blurts**

FLOURETTES (Idio Rank: 6.3)

Seemingly polite and conventional people who intermittently make offensive, fleeting Tourette's-like statements to catch people off guard. Flourettes aren't overtly crass on a day-to-day basis. They just enjoy peppering their conversation with unexpectedly rude comments to prove they aren't as tame as they seem. After offering sensitive, encouraging advice, for instance, a Flourette will change the tone of the conversation with an unrelated anecdote like: "This truck almost ran me over at the crosswalk today. I was so mad I almost pulled my tampon out right there and threw it at his windshield." Most Flourettes worry that people perceive them as being naïve or innocent and enjoy raising a few eyebrows to add a layer of mystery to their personalities.

BLURTS (Idio Rank: 6.4)

Children who say racially and religiously insensitive things by mistake. Most commonly, Blurts are white children who don't understand the semantic difference between "nigga" and its inappropriate counterpart. Trying to fit in at school, they say things like "Those are some hella dope kicks you got on, nig———." They discover their faux pas when they're punched in the face and suspended from school. Other Blurts embarrass their parents by mistaking older orthodox Jews with Santa. Blurts taking their first Communion might exclaim, "Jesus tastes good, like Sharkleberry Fin Kool-Aid!" Some Blurts shout out, "Look, she's having a baby," when encountering someone with a weight problem. Luckily, most Blurts outgrow these problems as they age.

11 | Sigmund Fruits

IN BRIEF: People who insist on telling you about their dreams

POPULATION SIZE: Common

GENDER: Male or female

HABITAT: Ethereal realms, IHOP

HOBBIES: Talking, taking a tiny breath of air, talking some more, wondering how to best describe the minotaur-grasshopper, taking another tiny breath, forgetting the point

IDIO RANK: 5.7

A Sigmund Fruit relating a dream

Overview

Most of us live in two worlds, the waking world and the subconscious world of slumber and dreams. People who know a Sigmund Fruit, on the other hand, live in three worlds. In addition to the waking world and the dream world, they often visit a realm known as hell, a frightening place where they're forced to listen to relentless chatter about someone else's dreams.

Sigmund Fruits are a unique breed of storytellers who make the mistake of thinking the subconscious dream world of ominous attics, giant tadpoles, and naked public speaking events is interesting to anyone other than their shrink. They fail to realize that the details that make dreams fascinating are the inexplicable parts. The reason shrinks charge so much is because nothing is duller than listening to someone else's dreams. Everybody feels let down at the end of *The Wizard of Oz* when they discover Dorothy was only having a dream. Imagine if the film opened with Judy Garland saying "Hey, let me tell you about this dream I had about talking scarecrows, monkeys, and an Emerald City."

The Difference Is Night and Day

In the hands of an accomplished author, dreams can be an exciting literary device. *Through the Looking-Glass* was allegedly inspired by dreams (and opium) and is compelling because Lewis Carroll took the time to get the details right. When Sigmund Fruits tell you their dreams, it's usually a stream-of-consciousness endeavor, devoid of forethought and the elements that make a story entertaining or meaningful. The dreams they relate have little in common with the written dreams one reads in novels that often utilize minimal language, a staccato writing style, and elements of suspense:

HOW MOST AUTHORS WRITE ABOUT DREAMS

I'm an archaeologist. I'm on a dig in Africa searching for ancient tribal remains. My guide speaks no English but is familiar with the grassy terrain. He has a necklace made from lion's teeth. While I'm digging, I feel his hand on my shoulder. I look up and see he is pointing at something. I sense that he is afraid. I follow his finger and notice the long, flowing grasses ahead have begun to part like the Red Sea in *The Ten Commandments*. . . .

HOW SIGMUND FRUITS TELL THEIR DREAMS

I am at this buffet at a restaurant and for some reason, I don't know why, all the food seems to have gone bad. Wait, no, the chicken is okay. I remember because I ate it, and it was good. The chicken was definitely good, but all the other food on the buffet had spoiled. I felt sick and told the restaurant manager, and guess what? The manager was David! Except he wasn't *just* David because later he turned into Maria, but I'll get to that part in a second. Wait. Now that I think about it, it wasn't a restaurant, but my old high school cafeteria and Shecky was there. And actually, I'd packed my lunch. I remember because I had my old Thundercats lunchbox and I had packed some chicken in a Ziploc

bag. I know the dream was in color because the chicken crust was like this
strange shade of brown. Oh, crap, I forget what happened next.

Sigmund Fruits in History

Sigmund Fruits have lived among us throughout history, though they have
never been properly studied or identified as a people. Jim Jones, the cult leader
whose followers committed mass suicide by drinking poisoned Kool-Aid, often
related his dreams to his "flock." Charles Manson was a Sigmund Fruit as well.

Going back further in time, Sigmund Fruits from the fourth millennium
B.C. in Assyria and Babylon often documented their dream lives on cuneiform
tablets. Historians believe that these ancient people were forced to write their
stories down by family and friends who couldn't bear to hear any more
dreamland tales about the Euphrates mermaid, slingshots, or hot brunettes
from rival dynasties.

In more recent times, the Surrealists all cite the dream world as a major in-
fluence on their work. A little-known fact is that Salvador Dalí's lover is responsible for the conception of the Surrealist movement. After waking every morning
at eight o'clock to the sight of that silly little mustache hovering over her, she
encouraged Dalí to paint his dreams of melting clocks and desert wastelands
instead of boring her with them. Surrealism was born.

PAGE EIGHTY-SIXERS (Idio Rank: 3.3)

Page Eighty-Sixers are laymen paparazzi who commonly spot people who look "just like" celebrities at the mall, church, and Applebee's. Page Eighty-Sixers point to random people they encounter in public and say, "Doesn't that person look just like Colin Farrell?" When in the presence of a Page Eighty-Sixer, several spottings are all but guaranteed. Most sightings are a bit confounding to friends since the aforementioned Colin Farrell look-alike is generally balding, cross-eyed, and in his late fifties. Page Eighty-Sixers who are less pop culture savvy further confuse friends by saying "Doesn't that girl over there look just like that woman on that TV show?"

Freud and Jung

Sigmund Freud and Carl Jung were the creators of dream therapy. Freud claimed that dreams are nothing more than subconscious wish fulfillment. He is clearly wrong. Otherwise, Sigmund Fruits would all dream of being booked at Madison Square Garden for the "I-Was-In-My-Room-But-It-Looked-More-Like-My-Childhood-Bedroom Spoken Word Dream Tour."

Jung, on the other hand, believed that the symbols found in dreams are shared by everyone in the collective unconscious. His work seems incomplete since obvious elements that inhabit dreams, like cheese fries, are not even mentioned in his journals. Freud and Jung had a public falling out after Freud insisted on recounting one of his own dreams about a Native American chief driving a go-kart to Jung before the latter had had his coffee.

The Seven Most Common Dream Elements:

1. Showing up at work or school naked.
2. Falling or flying.
3. Doing Britney against the washer while Matt Lauer masturbates into the dryer.
4. The bearded old Wise Man and the maternal Earth Mother.
5. Bacon, egg, and cheese biscuits.
6. Sausage, egg, and cheese biscuits.
7. Being chased (and dropping one of the aforementioned biscuits).

Things You Can Do to Silence a Sigmund Fruit:

Sigmund Fruits' insistence upon sharing every detail of their nighttime journeys can tear at the bonds that hold a relationship together. The dangers are real, but that doesn't mean Sigmund Fruits cannot be cured. Here are a few simple suggestions:

▶ Never let a Sigmund Fruit eat before going to bed. Sleeping with a full stomach can cause intense dreams for anyone.

▶ Tell the Sigmund Fruit you have a minor in psychology and interpret his dream by saying "Wow, you're *really* screwed up."

▶ Stoners often tape themselves to document their "profound" conversations. (The results are always guaranteed to be embarrassing.) Taping Sigmund Fruits and then playing their monologues back to them can sometimes help to alleviate their psychosis.

 HOMOFABS (Idio Rank: 7.9)

Similar to people who claim to not be racists by saying "I have lots of black friends," HomoFabs suggest that they're not homophobic since they watch *Queer Eye for the Straight Guy*. When put on the spot to defend a statement like "I just don't think gays should be allowed to take showers with straights in the military," they respond to accusations of homophobia by addressing their appreciation of *Queer Eye* as a safety net.

"I have no problem with gay people. I think Carson and the Fab Five are hilarious!"

When this doesn't work, HomoFabs sometimes offer a follow-up by claiming to love the song "Rocket Man." They know that the combination of the two could absolve anyone from homophobic accusations.

12 | The Other Soccer Moms and NASCAR Dads

IN BRIEF: The forgotten parent and relative demographics
IDIO RANK: Varies (see below)

A Soccer Lily with her daughter

Overview

Everyone is familiar with the term "soccer mom": conventional, suburban house-wives who pick their children up after school from soccer practice. They have an affinity for minivans and SUVs with *Child on board* or *My kid is an honor roll student* bumper stickers. Today, nearly fifteen years after the term was coined, most people recognize that the expression "soccer mom" was always much too general to have much sociological significance. The children of so-called soccer moms often don't even like soccer and play football, basketball, or even lacrosse instead.

Plus, most "soccer" moms would prefer being named for *their* activity of choice, not the sport their children happen to play. Further muddying the debate is the fact that the term "soccer mom" on the Internet has come to mean "a middle-aged, topless woman posing on her knees." In order to better understand the different types of moms in a more meaningful and sensitive way, here is a snapshot of the forgotten demographics.

The *Other* Soccer Moms

YOGA MOMS (Idio Rank: 2.8)

While they're waiting for their kids to finish soccer, basketball, or football practice, Yoga Moms spend much of their time in yoga class, drinking lattes at Starbucks, and fantasizing about what life would have been like in the city. Many Yoga Moms are artists and work on their own art projects while their husbands are at work during the day. Yoga Moms resent being called housewives. They do their best to defy the rigidity of the stereotype with their progressive beliefs and their openness to trying different stuff like Indian food or shopping at the new open-air mall. Yoga Moms resent more conventional soccer moms who vote Republican, shop at Wal-Mart, and don't tip the guys at Jiffy Lube well enough. They consider themselves to be more sophisticated than the other moms on the PTA and tune out the whispering of those who worry about their parenting abilities, given their subversive *Think globally, act locally* bumper stickers. Yoga Moms take pride in their children and try to teach them to be more open-minded than the other kids. They secretly resent the fact that their children play sports at all. They'd rather them paint, read, or try out for *Bye Bye Birdy*, but pretend to be supportive nonetheless.

TREADMILL MOMS (Idio Rank: 2.9)

The Treadmill Mom is an active career mom who doesn't have time for sports, save an occasional visit to the gym. She picks up her kids from soccer practice when time allows, but generally leaves it up to her husband or the resentful **Binoculars Mom** (the neighborhood busybody) across the street, who secretly curses her for having her values all mixed up. Some Treadmill Moms hire nannies. Nevertheless, most Treadmill Moms spend lots of quality cell phone time with their kids and even buy them their own phones when they turn five.

SOCCER LILIES (Idio Rank: 2.1)

Soccer Lilies are similar to soccer moms, only they have lesbian haircuts. After marriage and children, they simply stop worrying about their appearance, cut their hair short, and begin wearing lots of plaid, pleated denim, and pants with drawstring waists. Soccer Lilies are always very active parents and don't want to waste time worrying about fashion or makeup. Plus, as they'll attest, only superficial people waste money on expensive haircuts from Supercuts.

TENNIS MOMS (Idio Rank: 7.6)

Tennis Moms live off their husbands' wealth and resent accusations that nannies don't provide adequate parental instruction. They spend too much time playing tennis, socializing at the club, and sipping scotch to put in any extra hours with their children. They commonly miss out on Jimmy's games when recovering from Botox treatment.

VAN HAGAR MOMS (Idio Rank: 8)

Van Hagar Moms really dig hair metal and think soccer moms are a bunch of "uptight cunts." All Hagar Moms have cigarette purses, which never, under any circumstances, leave their grips. They try not to smoke too much in front of the kids but often expose them to the much more toxic secondhand fumes of aerosol hairspray. Van Hagar Moms confuse everyone around them since they call their husbands *and* their fathers "Daddy." Older Van Hagar Moms are sometimes called **Molly Hatchet Moms**.

Beyond the NASCAR Dad

OVERVIEW

It was only a matter of time before the media coined a term similar to "soccer mom" that applied to men. They came up with NASCAR Dad. According to public understanding, NASCAR Dads are Southern, God-fearing conservatives who always vote Republican, love racing, and think that rabbit tastes good on a cracker. Many worry the association with NASCAR isn't necessarily a good thing since people commonly joke that NASCAR is an acronym for Non-Athletic Sport Centered Around Rednecks.

Similar to the term "soccer mom," the "NASCAR Dad" moniker is largely a stereotype that's much too general to have any sociological meaning. NASCAR fans can be found anywhere and they're a much more nuanced group than they're often portrayed as being. Nevertheless, most *do* agree that rabbit tastes good on a cracker. Here's a snapshot of some of the less frequently acknowledged types of American fathers, including the NASCAR Dads.

LABONTE DADS
(NASCAR DAD TYPE A)
(Idio Rank: 5.1)

Labonte Dads are named for the clean-living Christian NASCAR driver Bobby Labonte, who drove the "Passion of the Christ" car in the Indianapolis 500. Labonte Dads are Southern conservatives who go that extra mile to raise a moral, respectable family. Cussing and drinking, they know, is for degenerates. The Christian way to burn off excess testosterone is to watch someone

A NASCAR Dad with his son

else drive a car around a track at 200 miles per hour. Labonte Dads always tuck in their Richard Petty T-shirts and don't allow smoking in their homes. Cigarette smoke damages the fur on the mounted deerhead in the Bible room. Labonte Dads watch the races on TV since all the tailgating at the speedways gets a little rowdy. After all, Jesus is a race fan, but he wouldn't want to be around all that drinking and hollering either.

SMOKE DADS (NASCAR DAD TYPE B) (Idio Rank: 7.9)

Smoke Dads relate intimately to the loose-canon NASCAR driver Tony "Smoke" Stewart, whose wild living and notorious driving style have earned him much notoriety. Smoke Dads vote Republican not because of morality and values but because they want the candidate who supports kicking the most ass overseas. When Smoke Dads get frustrated with their kids, they take a time-out. A Miller time-out. Nobody likes drinking alone, so sometimes they crack open a brewski for their kids. Why can't quality time be Miller Time? Smoke Dads don't mind picking up the kids after school one bit, though they're a little nervous about getting pulled over since they can never remember if they've had two beers or three. To be safe and less conspicuous, they drive the extra car since they haven't removed its muffler yet. Good parenting also involves showing the kids how to use the Stadium Pal bathroom bag, so they don't miss any valuable moments of the race.

GOLF DADS/BOWLING DADS (Idio Rank: 6.8)
Golf Dads and Bowling Dads spend the majority of their free time playing their respective sports. Both use these activities as a way to buy themselves time away from their families. Their plans often come back to haunt them, however, since their overstated love of golf or bowling dooms them to receiving sports-themed gifts on every given holiday and birthday.

SPEED-WALK DADS (Idio Rank: 7.1)
Speed-Walk Dads are the envy of all the other moms in the neighborhood. They're sensitive, athletic, look great in biker shorts, and appear to be the perfect fathers. They don't mind picking up their kids from soccer practice one bit. After all, Coach Sims sure does look hot in his gym shorts.

FUTBALL DADS (Idio Rank: 2.1)
Futball Dads are stay-at-home fathers who have grown tired of the joke about being a "soccer dad." They jokingly claim to be Futball Dads (the European name for soccer) because it sounds more manly.

Other Family Types

KITE-FLYING PARENTS (Idio Rank: 5.5)
Kite-Flying Parents are back-to-the-earth parents who would rather their children find creative ways to express themselves than play competitive sports like soccer. Painting the top of an umbrella with festive finger paints or making bird feeders out of pinecones and peanut butter are activities that are better suited for children. Kite-Flying Parents know that sports are divisive and can cause self-esteem issues. Children should be taught that everybody is a winner instead of being encouraged to defeat an opponent. Kids should get their exercise skipping, jumping rope, or swimming in the pond behind the vegetable garden. Kite-Flying Parents also have an aversion to coloring books, knowing that children should be encouraged to create their own magic worlds to color. Many write their own family theme songs to sing around the piano with choruses like "This family colors outside the lines, keep lovin' one another and we'll be fine, Yeah, yeah, bucko, we'll shine."

SPLINTERS (Idio Rank: 6.8)

Society has established rules of war. People who defy these laws are often charged as war criminals. Splinters defy the rules of breaking up. They're "break-up criminals." The Splinter's knee-jerk response to "I'm sorry, sweetie, but this isn't working anymore" is usually along the lines of "Oh yeah, well, you're a fucking whore" or "Good, you have a microscopic penis anyway."

Splinters know that if they don't make their mark with you romantically, at least they can leave you worrying about your "huge ass" or about how all your friends think you're selfish. After all, complimentary comments made by happily committed people are quickly forgotten. Tell someone they're horrible in the sack and, well, that can last a lifetime.

SPIN-THE-BOTTLE SISTERS, GATEWAY DRUG BROTHERS (Idio Rank: 8.2)

Spin-the-Bottle Sisters try to corrupt their younger siblings by getting them to play age-inappropriate games with their teenage friends. Gateway Drug Brothers prefer corrupting them by introducing them to cigarettes, booze, or the Ostrowsky kid down the block who makes fake IDs.

TWISTER UNCLES (Idio Rank: 8.7)

Twister Uncles are family members with shifty eyes and overly friendly hugs who discover their affectionate side when their cousins and nieces buy their first training bra. Whereas flirtatious grandpas are usually written off as being harmless, Twister Uncles sometimes require a thorough tongue-lashing from Cousin Willy.

WESTMINSTER DOG SHOW AUNTS (Idio Rank: 6.1)

Westminster Dog Show Aunts are of the same genus as Antiques Roadshow Aunts, Born-Again Brothers-in-Law, and Corner-You-So-I-Can-Babble-for-Two-Hours Uncles. All the aforementioned are beloved relatives whose sensibilities and lifestyles nonetheless confound others in the family. Westminster Dog Show Aunts are very helpful when it comes to picking the kids up from soccer practice, but before the children spend time with them, parents must first provide a disclaimer to explain their quirkiness: "We love Aunt Jenny, but she's a little bit different. In fact, that's why we love her."

DOG TRACK BROTHERS-IN-LAW (Idio Rank: 7.9)

Dog Track Brothers-in-Law consider it their role to show children how the world really operates. After all, children are no different from adults, they just know fewer cuss words and have a lower tolerance for booze. On the rare occasion that the children are left in their care, Dog Track Brothers-in-Law must be reminded that the kids can absolutely not smoke. And if a Dog Track Brother-in-Law plans on seeing Peggy, he must be reminded that she can't hold little Mickey, given what happened last time. Most are responsible enough to have the kids wait for them at the arcade should they need to swing by the track.

 ANTI-GENTITES (Idio Rank: 6.6)

Anti-Gentites are passive-aggressive Jews who date non-Jews to avoid commitment. They enjoy the solitary life and know that dating Gentiles is a free ticket to eternal singlehood. When things get too serious, they simply break things off, insisting they can only commit to Jewish partners. Most begin dropping clues about their families' strict sense of tradition on their third date and insist they cannot betray their wishes. After all, taking a Gentile out to dinner is okay, but holding hands with one in front of Aunt Barbara at a bar mitzvah is more risky than defying the Torah. Many utilize the C word (convert) to prevent the L word from ever being broached. Asking a semi-serious partner to convert is a surefire way to free things up so they can ask out that cute intern at the office.

13 | The Safeway Sage

IN BRIEF: Retired men who communicate using gender-based jokes, wife jokes, and corny one-liners like "Working hard or hardly working?"

POPULATION SIZE: Common

GENDER: Male

HABITAT: Grocery store parking lots, hardware stores, standing in the middle of the sidewalk

FAVORITE BOOKS: *Men Are from Mars, My Wife Is from a Black Hole*

IDIO RANK: 5.3

Overview

"Need a hand? My wife will be right out." Heard that one? Then you must know a Safeway Sage. Safeway Sages are retirees who are overflowing with life's wisdom and have an ample supply of one-liners and jokes for any occasion. Their preferred topics are marriage, lawyers, dizzy blondes, in-laws, feminists, PMS, and sometimes blacks or "Pollocks." Safeway Sages commonly take on part-time jobs bagging groceries at the Safeway or cutting keys at the hardware store after retiring. This helps them to stay active and provides them with an audience with whom to share their humor. Nevertheless, Safeway Sages can be found almost anywhere, except of course places like the café at Barnes & Noble, where the rock music is played too loudly.

The Great Communicator

Many older people have a habit of repeating themselves and Safeway Sages are no different. They relate the same familiar adages over and over to the delight of all of those around them. After all, a classic witticism like "I'm not getting old, my mirror is wrinkled" sounds fresh no matter how many times you've heard it. Safeway Sages who have mastered their delivery know the usefulness of the follow-through wink.

Many Safeway Sages only watch old Bob Hope movies or Sean Connery–era James Bond films. As a result, they fail to realize that puns about dizzy blondes screwing in lightbulbs haven't aged as gracefully as they have. When their wives punch them for crossing the line with their antiquated gender humor, most Safeway Sages just think their wives are playing the straight man role, a Dean Martin to their Jerry Lewis. Nonetheless, jokes that compare the usefulness of women and electric dishwashers can make people from a younger generation a tad uncomfortable.

Though Safeway Sages prefer letting others do the talking and throwing out one-liners in response, they do on occasion initiate conversation themselves. Their favorite topics are as follows:

▶ the outrageous prices people charge for fancy coffee
▶ that wacky weatherman
▶ Vanna White
▶ plumbing
▶ how "Oriental" food is pretty tasty after all

The Unconscious Collection

No matter where you live, or how far you travel, Safeway Sages inexplicably share the same set of catchphrases and jokes. Many people even wonder if they are simply running into the same guy over and over. They all seem to share

Popular Quotes from the Unconscious Collection

▶ "Working hard or hardly working?"
▶ "It's a small world, but I wouldn't want to paint it."
▶ "When you're over the hill, you start to pick up speed."
▶ "I pretend to work, they pretend to pay me."
▶ "With friends like you, who needs enemies?"
▶ "I have a photographic memory, I'm just out of film."
▶ "Actions creak louder than words."
▶ "Put that in your pipe and smoke it."
▶ "I'm pushing seventy—that's enough exercise for me."

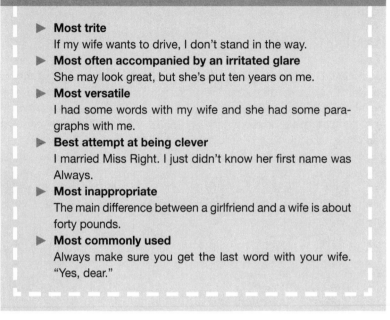

The Marriage One-Liner Hall of Fame

▶ **Most trite**
If my wife wants to drive, I don't stand in the way.

▶ **Most often accompanied by an irritated glare**
She may look great, but she's put ten years on me.

▶ **Most versatile**
I had some words with my wife and she had some paragraphs with me.

▶ **Best attempt at being clever**
I married Miss Right. I just didn't know her first name was Always.

▶ **Most inappropriate**
The main difference between a girlfriend and a wife is about forty pounds.

▶ **Most commonly used**
Always make sure you get the last word with your wife. "Yes, dear."

the same youthful flicker in their eyes and the same pair of unimaginably white sneakers. And after asserting "She calls me *sweetie* because she can't remember my name," all Safeway Sages recoil from their wives' exasperated pinches in the same way. How can Safeway Sages, no matter where one encounters them, be so alike?

As with Jung's collective unconscious, psychologists theorize that Safeway Sages all share access to something known in science as the **Unconscious Collection**. The Unconscious Collection is a mysterious assortment of witticisms such as "the check's in the mail" that Safeway Sages can borrow from without actually having to consciously give thought to their responses. The Unconscious Collection allows them to go on autopilot. Scientists believe this is one of the body's natural defenses against aging. It frees up brain activity that could otherwise prevent proper blood flow to the Safeway Sage's body.

Marriage One-Liners from the Unconscious Collective

The Safeway Sage's favorite topic is marriage. This is the area where they truly shine. On topics such as religion and the weather, Safeway Sages typically only have one or two standard responses on hand. When it comes to the topic of marriage, however, they have a wealth of jokes and one-liners to choose from. When you see a Safeway Sage mumbling to himself, chances are he's practicing his delivery of a marriage joke.

Premature Clichéing

Sometimes, people prematurely begin relying on the crutch of social clichés associated with Safeway Sages. **PremaGeris** (pree-muh-jerries), as they're known, begin running on conversational autopilot in their thirties or forties, saying things like "Look what the cat dragged in" instead of a simple hello. Though most people turn a blind eye to Safeway Sages, writing off their eccentricity as part of the generation gap, PremaGeris inadvertently alienate themselves from friends and family with their age-inappropriate rhetoric. PremaGeris who try to pick up women at bars using lines like "Hot enough for ya?" usually have limited success. PremaGeris who make marriage jokes like "Marriage is a very expensive way to get laundry done" often require the intervention of loved ones to ensure their own well-being.

 **Telemutes and Griffins**

TELEMUTES: (Idio Rank: 5.4)

Telemutes are people who call friends and family regularly but don't actually have anything to say. The typical conversation with a Telemute goes something like this:

> **You**: Hello
> **Telemute**: Hi
> **You**: Oh, hey. What's going on?
> **Telemute**: Not much, how about with you?
> **You**: Nothing much.
> **Telemute**: Me either.
> **You**: So what's up?
> **Telemute**: Nothing, really.

This introduction is then followed by thirty minutes of *you* trying to come up with something to say, since Telemutes are only capable of contributing a sporadic "oh" and "uh-huh" to the conversation. The only time they actually speak is when you try to get off the phone.

Escape is impossible since they're sure to block your hanging up with a follow-up question to your last statement, like "Really?" or "How do you feel about that?" to keep you on the line a tad longer. Tragically, the Telemute population is dwindling. Caller ID has rendered them on the verge of extinction.

GRIFFINS (Idio Rank: 6.0)

Named for talk-show icon Merv Griffin, Griffins are perhaps even more exhausting than Telemutes. Griffins are people who interview strangers at parties, weddings, and social events moments after meeting them. Griffins reveal little about themselves but quickly propel a rapid fire of questions to whomever is the subject of their attention. Where are you from? What do you do for a living? Is it fulfilling? Do you feel more secure with your body now that you've had the stomach stapling surgery? Would you say you're satisfied with the way your life is unfolding? Did Nanna Josie sufficiently nurture you when your biological mom ran off with the foreman from the road crew?

Griffins usually come in two types: (1) the earnest, introverted Griffin who feels uncomfortable in social settings and wants to avoid mindless small talk, and (2) the **Shit-Eating Griffin**, who smirks while he interviews you and tries to trick you into saying something hypocritical or embarrassing.

CATSCAN* Number 2

Mary Hart

Several years ago, a nonprofit group was founded in protest of the controversial talk-show personality and New Age musician John Tesh. The National Anti-Tesh Action Society (NATAS) believes that John Tesh is an alien and the group regularly organizes picketers to attend his shows. Anyone who has heard Tesh's music would be hard-pressed to deny their claims. NATAS has overlooked one important, overarching detail—namely, many believe that *everyone* involved with *Entertainment Tonight* is from outer space.

This brings us to our second CATSCAN, Mary Hart, an *ET* colleague of Tesh's who has been hosting the popular show for more than twenty years. Not only has the pixyish Mrs. Hart mysteriously not aged a day since she started on *ET*, she's spawned a crop of clones on similar celebrity magazine shows, such as *Extra!*'s Dayna Devon. Devon's physical similarities to Mrs. Hart are so striking, many believe she must be a pod person.

Hart's alleged biography goes something like this: She was born in South Dakota on November 8, 1950. After winning the Miss South Dakota crown, she went on to become runner-up in the Miss America Pageant. As a contestant, she realized her passion for being in front of the camera and pursued a career in broadcasting. Several national commercials paved the way to hosting *PM Magazine* and a short-lived spot as cohost of *The Regis Philbin Show*. In 1982, she earned her spot on *Entertainment Tonight*, which set the standard for the entertainment/celebrity magazine show. Given her huge success, she has since secured her investment in her own fame by purchasing a $1 million insurance policy. On her legs.

Mary Hart wins a unique spot as a "conversationally challenged" person (and possibly an alien) because of an event that took place in 1991. Dianne Neale, a former fan of *Entertainment Tonight*, inexplicably began suffering from seizures every time she watched the show. After realizing the connection, she was diagnosed as having a rare form of epilepsy called temporal lobe seizure. Doctors concluded that the sound of Hart's electronically transmitted voice was

triggering the seizures. Her treatment was simple: turn off Mary Hart. Dianne took her doctor's advice and was cured.

These are the facts. She doesn't age. She has spawned clones. She causes seizures. She's friends with Tesh. Could Mary Hart be a threat to the human species? Could *Entertainment Tonight* be an alien organization infiltrating the airwaves, covertly plotting to control each and every one of us?

Mary Hart is our CATSCAN Number 2. She is one of a kind (we hope) and defies classification.

IDIOSYNCROLOGY GROUP 3

The Fashionista and the Image-Obsessed

We live in an image-obsessed society, where people are overly concerned with their appearance. The bizarre world of cosmetic surgery, breast augmentation, tummy tucks, and Botox warrants a psychological study in and of itself. As anyone who has ever flipped through an issue of *Vogue, GQ,* or *Cosmo* will attest, fashion isn't always about clothes. It's about attitude, posture, being in shape, and embracing or defying one's age. All these factors play a role in one's personal style.

Understanding fashion sometimes comes in the details. Small things, such as how one accessorizes, can say a great deal about his personality. If you commonly wear shell necklaces and baseball caps, you probably like arena shows featuring Dave Matthews and Phish. If you accessorize with a sphinx broach, you're more likely than most to have gnome statues in your garden. If you're in your forties but still wear your high school ring, chances are you're a big fan of franchise steakhouses. If you wear a necklace that you call your love beads, Tom Robbins is probably your favorite author.

The wardrobe details people choose for themselves are usually an indication of how they want to be perceived. In part 3 of this book, we will unveil Idio Types that distinguish themselves from others with their fashion aesthetic and/or treatment of their bodies.

 This image indicates that more thorough research on this particular Idio Type is pending.

14 | The WB

IN BRIEF: Individuals of an adult age who REALLY identify with Bugs Bunny characters

POPULATION SIZE: Moderately common

GENDER: Male or female

HABITAT: The Warner Bros. Store, Times Square

TURN-ONS: Tweety Bird press-on nails, smart casual dress shirts with Foghorn Leghorn patches

IDIO RANK: 6.8

Overview

No one denies that the Looney Tunes cartoon series is a classic. Fans of the series, young and old, are everywhere. Daffy, Bugs, Foghorn, Porky, Taz, and Tweety have delighted us for years in classics like "The Rabbit of Seville," "Putty Tat Trouble," and "Duck Dodgers in the 24½ Century."

WBs get their name from the Warner Bros. franchise as they take their appreciation of the show to a whole new level. They believe that certain Bugs Bunny characters are apt representations of themselves, revealing inner secrets and magnitudes of depth about their own personalities. The true WB regularly wears Looney Tunes clothing and decorates his home with WB towels and shower curtains. Some even have WB tattoos. More extreme cases may even insist upon being called Taz or Foghorn.

What's Up, Doc?

During the holidays, the WB is the easiest person to shop for on your list. They collect WB drinking glasses, stuffed animals, and DVDs until their apartments become virtual shrines to the character of their choosing. Some take things a bit too far and frighten would-be lovers with their matching cartoon-themed bedsheets and underwear.

The phenomenon of the WB is particularly interesting since it seems to be unique to the Bugs Bunny franchise. Adults who accessorize with WB patches, baseball caps, ties, pocketbooks, and backpacks are considered to be perfectly normal. However, choosing to wear a matching hat and sweatshirt bearing the image of Papa Smurf, Aquaman, or the lion from *He-Man* would probably meet with social disapproval.

The Major Types

Though WBs who identify with Foghorn Leghorn, Bugs, Daffy, Tweety, and the Road Runner are not unheard of (see the chart on page 73), the two major types of WBs are known as Tazes (Tasmanian Devil fans) and MarvHeads (Marvin the Martian fans). These characters speak to a large cross section of the population, helping them to better express who they are as individuals.

THE TAZ

Tazes are people who turn any event into a party or, for that matter, any party into an event. Tazes feel a bond with the Tasmanian Devil because he represents chaos, spontaneity, and Epicureanism. Plus, they just *know* he'd be cool to drink a sixer with. In the cartoon, the Tasmanian Devil enters a room in a whirl of motion akin to a tornado, tearing conformity and order to shreds. This is how the Taz sees himself too, an unpredictable force who cannot be tamed.

B.O.BLIVIOUS (Idio Rank: 5.9)

People who are B.O.Blivious challenge the conventions of fashion by clashing what appears to be a clean and ironed look with a rank unkempt stench reminiscent of the Bally towel bin. Unlike the typical unkempt person who knows he's probably a little ripe but just doesn't care, people who are B.O.Blivious are completely unaware of the problem. *I'm successful and went to a good school*, they think. *There's simply no way I could stink*. On the occasion that their stench is called to their attention, they're generally pretty confused. To make light of the embarrassing realization, many respond by saying, "I'm just more European than you." Others say, "You know, in earlier eras women would rub their natural odor onto an apple before presenting it to a lover." It should be noted that few have much success with this courting ritual. Rumor has it that some famous B.O.Blivious people include Abe Lincoln, Colin Quinn, Paul Wolfowitz, the brunette Dixie Chick, Nicole Kidman, and Tim Russert.

In addition to WB patches and gear, all Tazes have bottle openers on their key chains. Opening someone's beer at a party is a great way to meet people. Some even carry a keg pump, just in case the need should ever arise. Like King Arthur pulling Excalibur from the stone, Tazes fantasize about pulling a keg pump from their Taz backpacks to save the party. Male Tazes love the E! channel and think breast implants are cool. Female Tazes love beef jerky and enjoy beating up chicks with breast implants.

The Taz is the quintessential free spirit, a rolling stone who cannot be contained, categorized, or confined. When caught cheating on a lover, the Taz just points to the tornado-clad character tattooed on his arm and says, "You can't cage the wind, baby. You can't cage the wind."

THE THUG TAZ

A subcategory of the Taz, known as the **Thug Taz**, relates intimately to the popular Looney Tunes character because they think he's a badass. Thug Tazes have volatile tempers and wear the Taz emblem to add a little edge to their appearance. When the Thug Taz puts a WB sticker on his Hummer, SUV, Jeep, or Camaro, he's issuing a warning of "Don't tread on me."

The Thug Taz's favorite pastime is trying to make eye contact with strangers. To the Thug Taz, eye contact is the go-ahead for a fight or at least some invigorating shoving. Thug Tazes spend much of their time in mall parking lots leaning against their cars while listening to Cypress Hill. Thug Tazes always wear exceptionally baggy jeans and, unlike traditional Tazes, they're not at all fond of being called "Taz." Many are disappointed to discover that Smith & Wesson has yet to manufacture a WB gat. After all, pistol-whipping someone with a Taz gun would be fucking dope.

(**Note:** Tazes who develop marijuana habits sometimes switch over to Fat Albert insignia.)

MARVHEADS

MarvHeads are people who identify intimately with Marvin the Martian. They see themselves as being eccentric and unique, just like the memorable character on the show. Like Tazes, MarvHeads are fond of WB gear and collect sweatshirts, air fresheners, and seat covers to represent their unwavering affection. MarvHeads are often social outcasts and relate to the character since they sometimes feel like they're also from another planet. All MarvHeads enjoy making their voices nasally and monotone and saying, "Have you seen my Illudium Q-36 Space Modulator, Earthling."

MarvHeads are notorious jokesters who love making prank phone calls or pretending that they picked the winning lotto numbers. Smacking a metal sign to trick others into thinking they've bumped their head is always a crowd-pleaser. Dancing like a robot at the company party delights everyone and ensures that the MarvHead is the center of attention.

Many MarvHeads feel Marvin doesn't get the respect he deserves since he's considered to be a peripheral WB character on the show. They show their loyalty by purchasing *Virginians LOVE MARVIN* bumper stickers and by visiting Looney Tunes chat rooms to meet other fans. Many point out that Marvin is the best character to collect. When you run out of things to buy, you can mix it up by purchasing stuff that features his sidekick dog, K-9.

MIXING CHARACTERS

Some WBs mix different characters into their wardrobe to wear all at once. More often than not, this is done out of practicality when a friend or family member simply buys them a T-shirt with the wrong Looney Tunes character by mistake. Other times, WBs blend different characters into their wardrobes to convey that their personalities are nuanced and emotionally complex. For instance, a Taz who wears a Tweety Bird baseball cap may be trying to communicate that he has a sensitive side. And a MarvHead who wears a Taz wristwatch may be trying to appear a little more fun or tough.

The Other WB Types

LOONEY TUNES CHARACTER OF CHOICE	WHAT THE WB IS TRYING TO COMMUNICATE
Bugs Bunny	I'm traditional and practical but know how to have fun
Foghorn Leghorn	I'm a Republican
Daffy Duck	I'm a connoisseur of life and often misunderstood
Sylvester	I may not be successful, but I'm a good person
Elmer Fudd	I like cupcakes
The Orange Cat That Looks Like Sylvester	I'm an artist and one of a kind
Tweety Bird	I'm beautiful, feminine, and I like to spoon
The Singing Frog	I'm gay but want to defy the *gays dress well* stereotype
Yosemite Sam	I sometimes go poo-poo in my sweatpants
Porky the Pig	My brother thinks it's funny to make fun of my weight problem with pig-themed gifts
Road Runner	I take pride in being an asshole
Wyle E. Coyote	I'm a conspiracy freak and think ACME is a symbol for Big Brother

More often than not, WBs who mix characters are simply trying to break from their routines. They wake up thinking, *You know, I just feel more like Porky today than Daffy,* and dress accordingly. WBs who discover that they feel more comfortable wearing Tweety Bird jeans after years of devotion to Sylvester products may suffer from identity crises. It should be noted that the habitual mixing of characters could be a sign of mental instability.

15 | Food Court Druids

IN BRIEF: Teenage Goths obsessed with fantasy role-playing games like Magic the Gatherer

GENDER: Male, female, or androgynous

HABITAT: Food courts, *Harry Potter* premieres, Goth night

FAVORITE MUSIC: Industrial music, The Cure, Misfits, Nine Inch Nails, Marilyn Manson, Wolfsheim, Alien Sex Fiend

HOBBIES: Smoking cloves in the JCPenney parking lot, demon-like hissing at squirrels and younger children

IDIO RANK: 6.7

Overview

Like much of today's youth, Food Court Druids (FCDs) spend a good deal of time hanging out at mall food courts and bookstore cafés. They are a special breed of Goths obsessed with fantasy role-playing games like Yu-Gi-Oh!, Lord of the Rings, and other games associated with orcs, dragons, and plate-mail armor-wearing alligators. They know that if pagan icon Aleister Crowley were alive today, he'd spend his afternoons playing fantasy games at the big table just outside Pizzeria Uno too.

Like most Goths, Food Court Druids often achieve an alternative fashion aesthetic by face powdering and wearing black clothing, black eye shadow, black nail polish and even black lipstick. Whereas traditional Goths find wardrobe inspiration from the Victorian and Edwardian periods, FCDs find inspiration from the Dungeons & Dragons Player's Handbook. They stare at its contents for so long they begin to think bat amulets, spiked boots, and smart casual vampire fangs can really pull an outfit together. Most FCDs think it would be really cool if they had no reflection in mirrors.

Food Court Druid Aliases

Food Court Druids feel alienated from an American society that they feel is arrogant, ignorant, and not accepting of people who look like zombies. Similar to the way many African Americans adopt Muslim names in protest of American culture, FCDs often assign themselves aliases that they believe more closely represent their identities. They draw from Celtic culture, pagan tradition, Greek mythology, and the Harry Potter series when choosing a name. Selecting a name can be a daunting task. Here are some examples of strong (and not so strong) names for the aspiring Food Court Druid:

Strong Aliases	Weak Aliases
Trafalger ShadowWalker	Cinnabon Warrior
Lord Tatzelwurm	The Lord of Jenkins Castle
Kobold Druid	Incarcerated Faerie
Wind Ghost	Razor Boomerang
Frilldora Darkness	Little Lord Fauntleroy
Vampyria II	Mistress Swampy
Shamanic Blademaster	Band-Aid Feyguard
Lex Divina	Rancid Coffin
Midnight Vixen	Tadpole Slaya

Knocking 'Em [Un]Dead with Their Sense of Style

Many Food Court Druids wear iconic religious symbols like Christian crosses, Egyptian ankh necklaces, Wiccan pentagrams, and of course Darth Maul T-shirts. Spiked necklaces, snakelike contact lenses, and dragon claw finger attachments are timeless classics that never lose their elegance. When feeling uninspired, FCDs pop *The Crow* into their DVD players for fashion tips. Many FCDs are into body piercing, especially now that the Piercing Pagoda just reopened right next door to Old Navy.

The Perfect Scare-Do

Food Court Druids have unusual hairstyles and use Manic Panic hair dye to add a little flair. In the eighties and nineties, they always chose black dye jobs, but now it's become fashionable to mix things up with brighter colors and/or vibrant streaks. Black still reigns, but other popular hair colors include Vampire Red, Shocking Blue, Deadly Nightshade, and Fuschia Shock. Bloody Sarcophagus Bestial Warlust Crimson is another popular choice.

A Diverse Cast

Many assume that all Food Court Druids automatically have the same taste in music, comics, action figures, and fetishistic dog collars. In reality, FCDs are a very diverse Idio Type with varied opinions and tastes. Some, for instance, prefer horror, cyberpunk, or sci-fi role-playing games to the fantasy genre. And though all FCDs enjoy Popeye's french fries, some think Wendy's spiced chicken sandwich is better tasting than Burger King's chicken Whopper.

Many Food Court Druids are computer whizzes who enjoy writing viruses or playing the online versions of role-playing games. FCDs who are into computers are often paranoid and think the government is tracing their steps. Nevertheless, they're a defiant group who know the army of blue-fleshed super soldiers that the CIA is producing shall not prevail!

Food Court Druid/Goth Fundamentals

As Food Court Druids are a subcategory of Goths, it's not surprising that they possess many cultural similarities. In addition to being obsessed with death, the color black, and The Cure, all FCDs and Goths share the following beliefs:

▶ Doc Martens and Kiss boots rule.
▶ Getting beat up by the soccer team is preferable to getting beat up by the football team.
▶ Cutting yourself with a protractor is pretty f'in cool.
▶ If I ever get married, I will register for a nice dragon claw chalice set at Mistress Divina's NecroMart.
▶ Fashionable pants and corsets should have at least four unused pockets, straps, buckles, or spikes.
▶ That chick Tonya who wears all that Abercrombie & Fitch stuff is a total bitch.

Food Court Druid FAQ

Are Food Court Druids Vampires?

Rarely. Truth be told, they do have appetites that are as ferocious as those of the bloodthirsty undead, but they generally hunger for McNuggets, Ho Hos, french fries and other finger foods that don't impede a game of Magic the Gatherer.

Are Food Court Druids Satanists?

VERY rarely. Food Court Druids are just of the opinion that the demons damned to eternal suffering in the fiery abyss imagined in *Hellraiser II* dress really cool. Most simply find it amusing to shock others. And other than the occasional carnage-filled rampage, FCDs tend to be pacifists. The nature-based pagan beliefs to which they commonly ascribe historically precede Christianity and celebrate the altruism of the cloven-hooved goat man.

The only people that *really* think Food Court Druids are Satanists are disciples of Pat Robertson and the people who produce *Dateline* exposés on the occult. Nevertheless, coming up with satanic nicknames for Food Court Druids like Demon Girl, Damien, or Rosemary's Baby can be a blast for anyone.

Are Food Court Druids on Drugs?

Rarely. Most are too dorky to score any of the good shit.

Why Do They Wear All Black?

Many Food Court Druids begin feeling alienated from others at an early age. In order to differentiate themselves and express their inner pain they begin dressing in black and listening to melancholy music. Other FCDs dress creepy hoping to scare people away from giving them wedgies. They think, *If I wear a skull ring with spiked teeth, maybe the jocks in homeroom will think I'm a witch*. Many have ongoing fights with their clueless moms, who insist on washing their black capes in hot water, which, needless to say, fades the demon pattern stitched into the fabric.

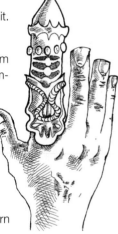

Dragon claw finger armor

Are Food Court Druids Gay?

Given Food Court Druids' refusal to conform to traditional gender roles and their love of fetishistic clothing, more close-minded types assume that they are all are gay. In reality, the jury is still out, as most FCDs are virgins. Their habit of carrying nunchakus and wearing dragon rings leaves them a small pool of lovers from which to choose. Plus, corset knots and the chore of undoing all of those excess boot buckles can further frustrate their attempts. FCDs who aren't virgins usually claim to be bisexual, but in reality most prefer drinking Slurpies and hand-painting goblin figurines to having sex.

Sometimes Food Court Druids are propositioned by more conventional people who are enticed by their alternative styles. FCDs repel such advances by saying "My true nature cannot be revealed to beings who aren't of my like kind." The mystical connotations of this statement are often lost on those who assume that FCDs are admitting to being dorks when they refer to their "kind." In studying their culture, we have discovered some helpful FCD dating tips to help facilitate the courting process:

Good Date Movie Rentals
Harold and Maude
The Crow

Bad Date Movie Rentals
When Harry Met Sally . . .
A Larry Bird documentary

Good T-shirt Imagery
Skulls, pentacles, dragons
Lord of the Rings decals
H. R. Giger, Jason

Bad T-shirt Imagery
jack-o'-lanterns
Lord of the Dance decals
Casper, Scooby-Doo

Good Date Locations
Goth night at a club
Graveyard with a six-pack

Bad Date Locations
Creed laser shows at the Omnimax
Bally to achieve a six-pack

Useful Food Court Druid Pickup Lines

▶ My chaotic 9th-level Dwarven Cleric has 96 hit points.
▶ Excuse me but I think you have some mustard or something on your cape.
▶ My mother sucks cocks in hell.
▶ I bet I've seen *Attack of the Clones* more times than you.
▶ Your dungeon or mine?
▶ Once you've had a teenage pagan, you never go back.
▶ Wanna come over, listen to some Rammstein, and fantasize about killing ourselves?
▶ How does a dinner at Red Lobster followed by a bloodletting ceremony sound to you?
▶ Wanna see my ten-sided dice?
▶ Is that makeup or are you just naturally corpselike?
▶ That padlock choker necklace sure goes well with your demonic contact lenses

16 | Chihuamos

(chi-wah-moes)

IN BRIEF: Gay men who accessorize with tiny dogs to help pull
their wardrobe together. The term "Chihuamo" is derived
from blending "Chihuahua" with "homo."

POPULATION SIZE: Common in large cities, moderately
common elsewhere

HABITAT: Peer groups where Jessica Simpson is considered a diva

GENDER: Male, transgender

SEXUAL ORIENTATION: Ranging from gay to very gay, depending
on the dog breed

IDIO RANK: Varies (see below)

Overview

Bulldogs, shih tzus, pugs, Jack Russell terriers, and other pint-sized to small dogs have long been the breeds of choice for most gay men. In fact, finding a gay man who owns a pit bull, rottweiler, or German shepherd can be a daunting task given their bias toward more modest-sized animals.

At its root, this preference for smaller dogs has its origin in the gay man's desire to keep his clothing clean. Adopting smaller breeds with daintier paws ensures less messy jumping and fewer footprint stains on one's wardrobe. And of course, as most gay men will attest, owning Labs and similar face-licking breeds is *so hetero* anyway. Owning a pure pedigree is not unlike wearing a Helmut Lang suit or a trendy silk shirt from Barneys. It shows good taste. Gay men who adopt small dogs as an extension of their wardrobe are known as Chihuamos.

Not surprisingly, the type of dog the gay man selects can reveal depths about his personality. Since the gay community is remarkably fractured and diverse, we've identified some of the more common subcategories below. In the process, we discovered surprising consistencies in the types of breeds each subcategory prefers.

The Muscle Mary (a.k.a. The Chelsea Boy) (Idio Rank: 5.2)

LIKELIHOOD OF BEING A CHIHUAMO: Very likely

Muscle Marys are gay men obsessed with achieving the perfect body. They spend hours at the gym lifting weights to secure a muscle-bound physique and the perfect six-pack. They're generally more interested in their appearances, creatine shakes, and debating Colin Farrell's sexuality than in engaging in cerebral conversation. Some have been known to jeopardize their health with muscle-building steroids. Midwestern women visiting New York or San Francisco for the first time are sometimes in awe of all the hot guys they encounter and must be informed of the truth. Muscle Marys never date one another. They're too competitive about their bodies for successful intermingling. Many Muscle Marys wear gym clothes throughout the day or dress like frat boys. Muscle Marys prefer **English Bulldogs** because the dog's enormous, muscle-bound physique closely resembles their own top-heavy builds. Both possess a strong appearance but are more prone to toppling over from their own weight than inflicting much harm.

Barbies (Idio Rank: 5.3)

LIKELIHOOD OF BEING A CHIHUAMO: Very likely

Barbies are gay men who define themselves as being transgender or are into cross-dressing and drag shows. Given the lack of understanding and sensitivity they find in rural communities, they generally prefer city life. Needless to say, renting *The Adventures of Priscilla, Queen of the Desert* at Cletus's Video Barn in Bratwurst, Texas, rarely wins them many friends. Barbies are very fond of Chihuahuas, Lhasa apsos, shih tzus, and any small breeds that can fit into a carrying bag or pocketbook. Many are appalled by the negative press Paris Hilton has brought to the dog-in-the-purse phenomenon.

The Guppie (Idio Rank: 2.1)

LIKELIHOOD OF BEING A CHIHUAMO: Moderate

Guppies (gay Yuppies) are go-getters with successful careers and expensive, smart casual wardrobes to match. They have type A personalities and some-times become Sugar Daddies to less successful mates. Similar to the way jet-setting straight businessmen prefer models, Guppies usually seek the company of Muscle Marys when dating. In order to appear professional, Gup-pies often feel the need to downplay their sexuality. They prefer Jack Russell terriers because they don't look "quite as gay" as other smaller breeds. Their confident temperaments and thin, sturdy frames are a perfect match for a Guppie who wants to maintain a more conventional style. Nevertheless, it does become annoying when people point at their beloved pet and say, "Look, there's the *Frasier* dog."

The Bear, the Cub, and the Otter (Idio Rank: 5.2)

LIKELIHOOD OF BEING A CHIHUAMO: Moderate

A Bear is a gay man who defies the well-groomed, Banana Republic–loving stereotypes often associated with gay culture in favor of a plump, hairy, and more "bearish" style. Bears tend to dress like construction workers, Hell's Angels, or lumberjacks, often growing beards to obtain a fuzzy and cuddly appearance. Bears avoid body waxing at all costs, have an inherent aversion to *Will & Grace,* and think the juice bar should serve mac & cheese with hamburger in it.

Cubs are younger Bears or Bears who are bottoms. Otters are smaller Bears with less body hair or closely trimmed beards. Knowing that having Chihuahuas and other overly petite breeds would inevitably clash with their large, huggable appearances, Bears, Cubs, and Otters find chows to be the ideal compromise. Chows are much larger and are always fuzzy, just like the typical Bear. Gay men who dig Bears, Cubs, and Otters tend to think Wilford Brimley is hot.

Twinkies (Idio Rank: 8.3)

LIKELIHOOD OF BEING A CHIHUAMO: Unlikely

Twinkies are young boy toys in their late teens or early twenties who have been initiated prematurely into the world of clubbing. Twinkies live recklessly, in-

SHINERS (Idio Rank: 2.7)

Remember the bathtub scene in *The Shining*? The part where Jack Nicholson embraces the seemingly young, beautiful (and naked) lady in room 237 only to discover upon closer inspection that she's actually a decomposing zombie? Heterosexual men who come into contact with Shiners often have a similar experience. Shiners appear fit, sexy, and downright desirable from behind in their form-fitting outfits and sportswear. Their hair is vibrant and flowing, and their bodies are shapely and scantily dressed. Men often hasten their pace to catch a glimpse only to realize that the object of their attention looks like an extra from *Dawn of the Dead*. She probably plays bridge with their grandmother. People commonly accuse Shiners of being vain or of not conforming to an age-appropriate dress code. Truth be told, most are simply getting revenge on the types of lecherous rejects who tactlessly stared at them when they were younger.

---

dulging in recreational drugs and casual sex, and they always have laissez-faire attitudes to match. Similar to the way rednecks make regular appearances on *Cops*, Twinkies tend to make a disproportionate number of appearances on *Dateline* exposés. Twinkies usually live at home with their parents or float from sofa to sofa and thus rarely have dogs of their own.

Pigs and Trolls (Idio Rank: 8.9)

LIKELIHOOD OF BEING A CHIHUAMO: Unlikely

Pigs and Trolls are the scourge of the gay community given their creepy dating and sexual habits. Pigs are sexual predators who hang out in bathrooms and other seedy locales looking for a quickie. They have unkempt, often unhealthy appearances and are on a first-name basis with the entire staff at the free clinic. Trolls are gay men in their fifties who look their age but try to score with younger, unattainable men. Most Trolls develop leathery skin from frequenting tanning salons and have beady eyes that never quite focus in on the people they're talking to. Providing proper care for a dog is a big commitment, and both Pigs and Trolls are way too busy watching porn and meeting new friends at baths to find the time. Nevertheless, they have occasionally been known to adopt fuzzy Lhasa apsos or shih tzus to use as sidewalk bait.

The DL and Gayngsta (Idio Rank: 7.4)

LIKELIHOOD OF BEING A CHIHUAMO: Very Unlikely

The DL (an abbreviated version of the "Down Low") is a gay male who claims to be straight but nevertheless frequents gay clubs and bathhouses to score gay sex. Many DLs have families and claim to be happily married. They keep their sexuality a secret in order to sustain their marriages and careers, or to save face with closed-minded friends and family who would not be accepting of their gay lifestyles. Given the lack of acceptance many gay black men encounter within their own communities, the Gayngsta is a common subcategory of the DL found in primarily black neighborhoods. Gayngstas must be careful to always hide their house music collections in Wu-Tang Clan CD cases to ensure their safety when encountering Bloods and Crips. DLs and Gayngstas are unlikely to be Chihuamos. They avoid adopting small dogs in favor of tougher and larger breeds like pit bulls and rottweilers in order to keep their secrets intact.

How Gay Is Your Dog?

DOG GAYNESS METER

★★★★★★	so gay they can fly
★★★★★	as gay as a three-dollar bill
★★★★	exceptionally gay
★★★	pretty doggone gay
★★	moderately gay
★	a tad gay

Note: Tying a bow to a breed will bump it up a level.

Basset Hound ★   Jack Russell Terrier ★★★

Shih Tzu ★★★★★

Chihuahua ★★★★

Schnauzer ★★★

Shar Pei ★★★★

Pug ★★★

English Bulldog ★★★★

Huskie ★★★★★
(lesbian stars)

Miniature Dachsund
*0 stars; they're so gay
they're hetero*

Scottish Terrier ★★★

French Bulldog ★★★★★

Bull Terrier ★★

Chow Chow ★★★

17 | Unitards

IN BRIEF: People who walk around in normal society dressed in the full uniform of their favorite sports team

GENDER: Male or female

POPULATION SIZE: Common, except at the Gap

HABITAT: "The street" (even if the street they're referring to is "Deer Hoof Lane")

HOBBIES: Sony PlayStation basketball and other sports that don't soil your sneaks

IDIO RANK: 5.6

Overview

Ever since Run-D.M.C. secured a smash hit with the classic song "My Adidas" back in 1986, urban fashion has become more and more about brand-name recognition. Adidas has long been a popular favorite, but in recent days brands like FUBU, Rocawear, Ecko, and Phat Farm have cornered the market. Given hip-hop's longtime obsession with basketball jerseys and sports gear, it's not surprising that the seemingly disparate worlds of sports and fashion have merged. Nowadays, people often opt for Detroit Pistons or Atlanta Braves insignia instead of the Tommy Hilfiger logo. All the aforementioned brands even have their own jersey lines. These days, magazines like *Vibe* are virtually indistinguishable from *Sports Illustrated* as they're both filled with people in jerseys.

The Unitard is a sports fashion aficionado who takes his love of sportswear to an extreme level. Unitards not only wear team jerseys but also accessorize with baseball caps, sweats, jackets, and even boxers, all with their NBA and NFL logos prominently displayed.

Much of America's youth have found empowerment in the successes of their sports heroes and enjoy wearing team gear to show respect.

Plus, many enjoy emulating the styles of 50 Cent, P. Diddy, and Ludacris, who often wear sports jerseys onstage.

To Unitards, wearing sports gear illustrates that you're a bad mofu who shouldn't be fucked with, just like that streetwise gangsta Will Smith. Unitards who want to present a thug image mix things up a bit by wearing a do-rag beneath their A's or Spurs caps. Wearing sports gear is a logical choice for Unitards who are into the thug life. After busting a cap, you never know when you might want to shoot a few free throws.

What's All the Confusion?

Since Unitards always look like they're getting ready to do some layups or kick a field goal, it's not surprising that they're often mistaken for sports stars. To help distinguish themselves from the actual players, they insist upon only wearing dramatically oversized clothing. Nevertheless, when people encounter a Unitard in Lakers gear on the subway or at the Bed Bath & Beyond, they sometimes do double takes and wonder, *Is that Shaq?* Actual sports heroes who wear their gear outside of games often create a similar confusion. They get stuck answering questions like: "Aren't you Jay-Z? That last joint you put out, dawg, was off the hook."

When sitting next to a Unitard on a train, it's not a good idea to ask him for his autograph, even if you're a big fan of the team he appears to be representing. Most emulate the street-smart posturing of rappers and prefer not to be spoken to. And remember, it's really a long shot that you'll run into a sports hero who wears his uniform off the court.

Common Questions People Have About Unitards:

I sometimes see people dressed like basketball referees. Are they Unitards?
No. They're Foot Locker employees.

I asked a Unitard I met at Books-A-Million if he was a player, and he said yes. What's the deal?
Most likely he thought you said "playa."

When Unitards gesture with their hands and make horizontal peace signs, are they practicing sports signals to be used in a game?
Probably not. The hand gesturing done by Unitards is usually associated with hip-hop culture.

Should I offer the Unitards I meet Gatorade? Maybe they're thirsty?
This is not recommended.

I notice that the rims on Unitards' baseball hats are never bent. Is there a reason for this?

Yes, bent rims are for frat boys who listen to Counting Crows. Unitards know that shit sucks. Plus, if you don't bend the rim, you can always return your hat to the store should your team go through a slump.

What are the stats on Jay-Z? Is it true that he was a first-round draft pick for the Celtics in 2002?

Um. No.

Do Unitards come in all ages?

Yes. Though Unitards are usually of the twenty-something set, some have been known to wear sports uniforms well into their forties and beyond. Nevertheless, many older Unitards begin wearing golf outfits instead. Golf gear is smart casual for the Unitard and shows that they've matured.

What about people who wear NASCAR outfits? Are they Unitards?

Yes. NASCAR outfits are mainly for white people who enjoy Unitard fashion but don't want to be called "wigger" by the fellas at Earl's saloon. NASCAR fashion is growing in popularity, though, and is becoming more common among blacks, Latinos, and other minorities. Curiously, field hockey gear is yet to catch on.

Can women be Unitards?

Absolutely. They're just not as good at it.

COWGRRRLS (Idio Rank: 3.7)

In the popular book *Even Cowgirls Get the Blues*, author Tom Robbins envisions a sexually liberated cowgirl ranch filled with beautiful women who love riding horses almost as much as they love sex. Obviously, the beautiful cowgirls that men dream of meeting are about as common as mermaids. Sure, some women *occasionally* wear cowboy hats. And women sometimes dress in western gear on Halloween. But generally when a guy sees a girl in a cowboy hat—and here's a news brief for those on the slow side—she's a lesbian. Most likely she can kick your ass. Straight cowgirls don't exist outside of Mennen commercials. Cowgrrrls, on the other hand, are on the butchy side and can be found in any bar in the country that has a pool table and some Melissa Etheridge on the jukebox. Cowgrrrls are to lesbianism what leather wearers are to gay men.

18 | Gym People

IN BRIEF: The eccentric cast found at that breeding pool of
dysfunction known as the gym

GENDER: Male, female, or humanoid

HOBBIES: The Atkins diet, The South Beach Diet, The Fried
Food and Purge Diet

IDIO RANK: Varies (see below)

The Stretchibitionist (1.1)

Overview

At one time or another, most people have belonged to a gym. Having a membership to Bally or Crunch has become such a way of life for most Americans
that we no longer stop to think about how unusual wanting to go to the gym is
in the first place. First of all, there's the music. When it comes to workout-
friendly pop, there are songs with infectious melodies and songs with melodies
that infect you. Gyms only play the latter type. Remixed with a techno beat. Bad
music helps prevent the gym from getting too crowded. The typical gymgoer
can only endure the first twenty minutes of the extended remix of a Janet Jack-
son song before bolting.

Then there's the smell. Dirty towels aside, the aroma of Swiss cheese, egg,
and chuck roast sweat is inescapable since everyone is on the Atkins diet.

Running outside, playing sports, eating healthy, and simply staying active
are all one needs to stay in good shape, but most people join gyms anyway because of the weight machines. After all, having bulging pecs and a six-pack is
imperative given the strenuous physicality of most people's lives. You've got to

be ripped and muscular to sit at a desk all day. Especially if you're going to be on your feet at happy hour.

Though some people admittedly join gyms for health reasons, the vast majority of gymgoers are more concerned with simply looking good. Not to mention the fact that sweating alongside people with nice bodies while they're panting away on the treadmill can be quite a rush. Gym culture has even spawned its own set of gender-specific adjectives brimming with sexual tension:

Women want their bodies to be:	Men want their bodies to be:
toned	ripped
taut	cut
tight	rock-hard
trim	bulging

The Gym Subcategories

Since most gymgoers primarily work out to look good and increase their sex appeal, they fit quite naturally alongside the Fashionista. Like the office, the gym is a ripe breeding ground for eccentricity. Here are the primary types that inhabit today's typical gym.

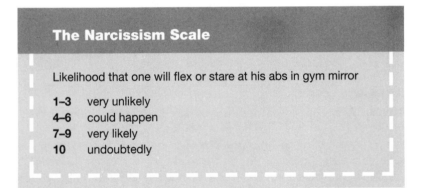

The Narcissism Scale

Likelihood that one will flex or stare at his abs in gym mirror

1–3	very unlikely
4–6	could happen
7–9	very likely
10	undoubtedly

THE HUMANOID (Idio Rank: 7.1)

You've seen him. He enters alone and the ground shakes as he passes. He's the humanoid. He weighs three hundred pounds and is too muscle-bound to move any part of his body other than his neck, legs, and fingers. His workout belt is duct-taped from snapping off one too many times. He has a vein above his left eye that looks like it could burst at any moment. Rumor has it, if you tickle him just beneath the belly button, he'll giggle and give you candy, but we wouldn't recommend it.

Narcissism Grade: 10

THE SCREAMER (Idio Rank: 7.2)

The Screamer could be on his first rep or his two hundredth. Either way, his roar will resonate throughout the gym, guaranteed. Though thorough research on the Screamer is pending, experts have suggested that steroids damage the cochlea, and Screamers simply don't realize they can be heard out in the parking lot.

Narcissism Grade: 7

MUSCLE MARYS (Idio Rank: 5.2)

Muscle Marys (see Chihuamos) have enormous torsos that are matched only by their enormous addictions to steroids and designer gym pants. Most prefer working out in gay-only gyms that have a steam room.

Narcissism Grade: 10

SPOTTERS (Idio Rank: 7.3)

Spotters think the gym is the ultimate singles' club. They do extensive detective work to discover which gym has the highest female-to-male ratio and are sure to join the winner. Spotters get their name from their most commonly used pickup line: "Need someone to spot you?" Others try to assist women who are weighing themselves on the scales by reaching over their shoulders to help them adjust the slider properly. Since most gymgoers catch on to what Spotters are up to pretty quickly, this Idio Type is often forced to prey upon the unsuspecting new girl. He shuffles up beside her nonchalantly to give her a good look at his pecs. The Spotter's Motto: To prevent injury, new female members always need to be instructed on how to operate the Nautilus machines. Provided they don't have cellulite.

Narcissism Grade: 8

The Top Pickup Lines Used by Spotters

▶ Can I spot you?
▶ I'm not macking, but have you ever kicked it with someone who's in peak physical form?
▶ You look like you could use a protein shake and a Clif Bar.
▶ I've got dumbbells, the new Pink disc, and showers back at my place.
▶ Let me adjust that seat for you.

THE STRETCHIBITIONIST (Idio Rank: 6.9)

It's unclear if the Stretchibitionist works out at all. The makeup she insists on wearing doesn't run, and she never seems to break a sweat. (The droplets of moisture seeping out of her catsuit cleavage don't count since they're usually self-applied.) She simply looks too fresh and clean to have spent much time on the Climber, which is exactly the idea since Stretchibitionists only go to the gym to show off their bodies and get attention.

Stretchibitionists get their name from their tendency to stretch suggestively in highly visible areas of the gym. They usually set up shop in front of the tread-mills and begin contorting their bodies in highly erotic positions until everyone on the floor has noticed them. Some Stretchibitionists prefer rolling around inti-mately with a medicine ball.

Stretchibitionists are generally of the post-thirty set and take great pride in their surgically enhanced bodies. Those who do actually work out prefer using the machines that make them appear ready to be mounted. Many walk around the locker room topless to show the ladies what their boyfriends were ogling.

Narcissism Grade: 10

The Stretchibitionist Thirty-Minute Workout

THIGHS/BACK/ABS

The Spread (see illustration 1.1) In a seated position, spread your legs as wide as they can humanly go. Slowly arch your back toward the floor behind you while pushing your chest outward. For added effect, inhale and exhale deeply to make your chest rise and fall. (5 minutes)

(1.2)

LEGS/THIGHS/CALVES/BACK

The Canyon (see illustration 1.2) Similar to the Spread, but done standing up. Spread your legs into an inverted V shape, bend over slowly and attempt to touch the floor. Hold the position and refrain from making eye contact with others; *you don't want any young stallions to shy away from peeking*! Ideally the view of your cleavage will create a canyonesque visual for everyone watching. (5 minutes)

ARMS/KNEES

The Feline (see illustration 1.3) Place your elbows and knees on the floor and move backward and forward on your mat in a seductive catlike crawl. Don't forget to push your lips out into an alluring pout. They need to be stretched too! (3 minutes)

PELVIS (GOOD FOR YOURS AND HIS)

The Thrust (see illustration 1.4) Sit on the mat with your arms behind you, your legs spread at forty-five degrees, and your knees bent. Using your arms and legs as support, elevate your back and butt off of the mat. Dip your butt slightly toward the mat and then slowly thrust your pelvis forward and upward. Repeat. When performed correctly, you (and your intended audience) should both feel stiff. (3 minutes)

(1.3)

(1.4)

BUTTOCKS/BACK

The Peacock (see illustration 1.5) Place your hands against the wall and position your butt high in the air, like you are about to be frisked. With any luck you will be! Move butt in a clockwise motion. Should anyone lose interest, begin moving butt in a counterclockwise motion. (3 minutes)

CARDIOVASCULAR AND SILICONE STRENGTHENING

The Pamela Why wait for a machine? Simply run in place to work up a sweat. Be creative and mix it up with some jumping jacks or grab a chair and do some *Flashdance* moves. (8 minutes)

COOL DOWN

The Narcolepsy Lie on your back with your legs slightly akimbo in a rested position. This helps facilitate the illusion that you are sleeping, drugged, or dead. In no time, they'll be thinking, *Gee, she sure would be easy to take advantage of.* (3 minutes)

(1.5)

All done!

SETWORKERS (Idio Rank: 2.9)

Some companies provide corporate gyms as an added perk for their staffs. This facilitates the health and livelihood of their employees and ensures increased productivity and morale.

The SetWorker has no interest whatsoever in working out but agrees to do some weight sets with his superiors as a way of brownnosing. SetWorkers know that in order to climb the corporate ladder they need to work out on the company Climber. Playing handball with Mary or running next to George on the treadmill for twenty minutes can improve the odds of getting a raise much more than working overtime ever will. Many bosses wonder, *If he doesn't even have the motivation to use the free NordicTrack, why should I trust him with the Clannaster account?* Others may consider non-gymgoers to be weak, or worse, liberals and communists. Should your boss suggest, "What say we do some reps after you finish reformatting the DCFS referral form?" the correct answer is usually yes.

Narcissism Grade: 2

THE SPY-MASTER (Idio Rank: 9.3)

The Spy-Master is not at the gym to work out. He's there to hang out in the Nautilus room next to the weight machines that are popular with women. Specifically the Thigh Master. Since men never use this machine, the Spy-Master is always guaranteed a good show. They sit on another machine close by and pretend to be cooling down. When no one is using the thigh machine, they swing by the water fountain to avoid being too obvious.

Narcissism Grade: 3

CARETAKERS/BARNACLES (Idio Rank: 6.4)

Caretakers and Barnacles are gymgoers who distinguish themselves by always, relentlessly, unquestionably, being at the gym, no matter what. Regardless of when you arrive, or what day of the week you choose to work out, the Caretaker is sure to have just beaten you out of the locker room and onto the machines.

Barnacles, on the other hand, are a special type of Caretaker who are always, unquestionably, relentlessly using the gym's most popular machine. No matter when you get there, you have to wait for them to finish or settle for a less intense workout on the bikes.

Do the Caretaker and the Barnacle have jobs? Are they staff? Are they undercover cops? How can they always be at the gym? The answer to each of these questions is quite simple. Like the Tao, they simply are.

Narcissism Grade: 7

THE TRENDSWEATER (Idio Rank: 3)

Trendsweaters are pretentious gymgoers who take pride in their ability to discern what's cutting edge in the world of working out. They have subscriptions to fitness magazines and keep their eyes on the bestseller lists to see what diet and workout books are hip. Trendsweaters knew that Pilates was a cool way to get in shape . . . *in like two thousand fucking three*. Now, Yogalates is the way to stay in shape fashionably. After all, Gwyneth stays in shape doing Yogalates.
Narcissism Grade: 7

PACKERS (Idio Rank: 7.3)

Packers get their name from their tendency to work out in, well, packs. They have matching lifting belts, workout gloves, and bandannas, and combined are the size of Green Bay's offensive line. Packers are always found in the free-weight room hovering territorially by their favorite weight bench. They believe that using the Nautilus machines is gay. Packers are extremely boisterous and usually have New York accents, even when they're from Kansas. They arrive together and take turns lifting, flexing, and glaring at women. Many Packers read copies of *Creatine Digest* while waiting their turn on the bench. Unless your boobs and hair color are fake, you'll more than likely be taunted with dirty looks should you try to "work in" on their preferred equipment.

Packers have their own unique exercise language. They say things like, "Yo, take another quarter off my press. I'm gonna flush my delts with more negative reps." Similarly, Packers also communicate using their own unique sexual lingo: "Yo, if I was to fling a nut at those headlights, you think they'd shatter?" No one is quite sure what either of these statements means, but the latter is usually accompanied by high fives.

Packers enjoy snickering at the pale, scrawny kid (see Street Shoes) who has to read the lifting instructions on the machines. They know that when their quads are ripped and burning, kicking his ass in the parking lot can be a great way to cool down.
Narcissism Grade: 8

THE POWER COUPLE (Idio Rank: 5.8)

Similar to the way all high schools have a popular cheerleader/football player couple, all gyms have a Power Couple. They always work out together and are inhumanly fit. Not surprisingly, they never sweat since both have successfully banished all socially unattractive genes from their gene pools following a millennium of meticulous breeding.
Narcissism Grade: 7

THE TOWEL ZEALOT (Idio Rank: 7.1)/NO-TOWEL RONNY (Idio Rank: 7.5)

The Towel Zealot doesn't usually sweat that much, he just enjoys scrubbing down the machine with his towel when he's done. For half an hour. A clean machine, he knows, is a machine that you can see your face in. Plus, the circular scrubbing motion is good for the biceps. No-Towel Ronny, on the other hand, does sweat a lot, but he wipes the machine down with his baggy V-neck wife beater. Which is already sweaty.

Narcissism Grade: 2

STREET SHOES (Idio Rank: 4.3)

Gymgoers known as Street Shoes have made a habit of avoiding gyms because they had some unfortunate experience back in high school involving towel-snapping or a nickname like "mole girl." In their twenties, they realize that playing drums for The Sullen Fringes isn't really keeping them toned and decide they need to get in better shape. Since most haven't been back to a gym since their life-scarring experience in school, they're unaware of core gym etiquette and end up wearing walking shoes, baggy indie rock T-shirts, and cutoffs. Some get yelled at for failing to wipe down a piece of equipment, or for not signing up for a coveted machine before using it. Others are horrified to find their cigarettes, wallets, and purses stolen from their lockers when they carelessly leave the combination sticker on their locks. Most are too timid to venture beyond the Nautilus room and master one or two machines before calling it quits. They last about six months before they become intimidated by the other longtime gymgoers or Tony.

Narcissism Grade: 3

TAE KWON JOE/TAE KWON HOE (Idio Rank: 6.2)

Tae Kwon Joe and Tae Kwon Hoe are narcissistic martial arts aficionados (usually of non-Asian descent) who take pride in their mastering of Tae Kwon Do, Tai Chi, and karate. They enjoy showing off their Tai Chi moves in lieu of stretching and stand abnormally erect since good posture is a sign of inner peace. Many meditate in a lotus position before beginning their workout. They offer a moment of silence to The One before doing their arm curls. Many keep their fingers crossed that the Dalai Lama will publish an abs book.

Narcissism Grade: 10

Idio Fashion Pictorial

Asiatrash
Asian women with trendy, over-the-top fashion aesthetics. Similar to Eurotrash.

(Idio Rank: 4.1)

Holidorks
People who make a habit of wearing holiday-themed clothing.
Preferably battery-powered, holiday-themed clothing.

(Idio Rank: 5.3)

Randys
Happy-go-lucky men who wear suggestive and/or raunchy T-shirts.
(Idio Rank: 7.7)

Skants
Women with shapely butts who *always* wear spandex pants.
(Idio Rank: 5.5)

Animal Accessorizors
People who bring their ferrets, snakes, and iguanas everywhere with them.

(Idio Rank: 6.3)

Cowboyees/Cowgizzles

African American men and women, respectively, who are obsessed with cowboy culture.

(Idio Rank: 5.1)

Perpendiculoids
People who maintain abnormally erect posture to look confident,
healthy, and fashionable.

(Idio Rank: 5.1)

Poppies
Sinewy, muscular hippies with toned physiques reminiscent of Iggy Pop.

(Idio Rank: 6.4)

Molly McButters
Trendy twenty-something women who dress like grannies.

(Idio Rank: 6.3)

Foremen
Smart casual rednecks.

(Idio Rank: 5)

African Amerigoths
Black Goths.

(Idio Rank: 7.1)

Randy Constan
(a.k.a. Peter Pan)

Some people model their style after Sid Vicious. Others opt for a vintage look, preferring a retro, Jackie O flair. Others think P. Diddy or J. Lo are stylish and pick up fashion cues from them.

Randy Constan bases his dress style on the wardrobe of Peter Pan.

A connoisseur of the green velvet leotard, Constan identifies intimately with the mystical Peter Pan character and goes so far as to dress like him on a regular basis. Though he admits his fascination with Peter Pan outfits (which he mostly makes himself) is a bit "fetishy," he claims that his intent is mainly to look androgynous:

> "Although Peter Pan is definitely a boy, to me this character is perfectly asexual, and in his eternal childhood rejects the idea of growing up."

Randy is a middle-aged computer programmer who lives in Florida. His business card states "Guitarist, Inventor, Engineer, Eternal Child," illustrating his large array of interests and talents. He is also a devoted Christian and has started his own church called Through the Cracks Ministries, devoted to acceptance and a liberal interpretation of the Bible.

In addition to his fascination with Peter Pan gear, Constan is also fascinated by "clothing styles of other times and places in history." On his Web site, Pixyland.org, he's also shown dressed as Little Lord Fauntleroy and Gainsborough's famous Blue Boy (the latter is pictured here and based upon the photo of his delightfully, frightfully detailed outfit). Randy's classic bowl-cut hairstyle accentuates his androgyny.

Despite his claim to be "pixyish, and unencumbered by notions of what is and is not permissible for boys," Constan is looking for a female companion. A "Tinkerbell," as he calls his unfound soul mate. Physical attraction and turn-ons (which he call "sparkles") are important, but Constan claims that "friendship,

common life interests and goals [are] the basis for a really lasting relationship."
However, he's not above being "knocked senseless by a cute Pixie," and her
magic "Pixie Dust," should the right Tinkerbell come along. Constan is definitely
very light on his feet; he's even pictured in flight on his "fashion" page online.
Nevertheless, he insists on his Web site that only Tinkerbells and Wendys can
win his heart (sorry, Captain Hook).

Visit him online at www.pixyland.org.

The Passionate, the Obsessed, and the Kinky

Passion, obsession, and sex are three forces that are understandably intertwined. Any discussion of obsession has to begin with sex, since it ranks so high on most people's priority scale. From Plushies[1] to feet fetishists to people who think The Rock is sexy, people's sexual predilections could fill the shelves of the Library of Congress. They'd have to add a wing. Nevertheless, many overarching consistencies exist when it comes to identifying groups of people in more meaningful ways than simply as heterosexuals or homosexuals.

Though sex is something most of us enjoy, many people are obsessed with more tangible things in life like their stamp collections, music, work, or breeding ferrets. More cerebral individuals sometimes become passionate about their political ideologies, understanding the nature of God, or deciphering the bad writing/good sales dichotomy of *The Da Vinci Code*.

When people become overly fervent about something in life, it can become disruptive and dysfunctional. Part 4 of this study profiles some commom Idio Types whose eccentric hobbies, beliefs, and love lives distinguish them from others.

 This image indicates that more thorough research on this particular Idio Type is pending.

[1]These are people who have stuffed-animal fetishes.

19 | Kristen Kringles

IN BRIEF: Women who are obsessed with Christmas year-round

GENDER: Female

Population Size: Moderately common

HABITAT: Ornament/snow-baby/tinsel stores

HOBBIES: Collecting snow globes, making paper-bag reindeer puppets

FAVORITE BOOKS: *The Leadership Secrets of Santa Claus; Red Jacket, White Beard, Rainbow Heart*

IDIO RANK: 7.5

Overview

If you make a habit of swinging by Lydia's Great American Christmas Store once a week in April, chances are strong that you're a Kristen Kringle. Kristen Kringles adore Christmas and the tinsel and gumdrop feelings they associate with the season. Candy-colored memories of Christmases past and the anticipation of joyful seasons to come provide them with a sense of peace unlike anything else in their lives. Most Kristen Kringles use the term "Christmassy" to denote extreme feelings of joy.

The Early Bird Catches the Snow Elf

Unlike most people, who start seriously preparing for the holiday as soon as the tree goes up in their homes, Kristen Kringles begin their preparations immediately after the tree from the past Christmas is taken down. It's never too early to begin thinking about next year's gifts, and there are always plenty of stockings to knit and porcelain Frosty the Snowman figurines to paint. Plus, Rite Aid's prices on Christmas doves and candy canes right after the holiday can't be beat. The Christmas lights, decorations, and Santa statues Kristen Kringles buy start to accumulate with time, but they always designate a room in the house as the Christmas room. It's a magical place.

Are They Religious?

Contrary to popular belief, Kristen Kringles are not religious and rarely decorate their homes with Christian iconography or wear *Jesus Is the Reason for the Season* pins. Kristen Kringles find fulfillment in the *secular* traditions of the holiday and usually avoid church until December. That's when the pageants begin and things really start happening!

The Joy of Children

Christmas is best enjoyed in the company of children. Kids feel the excitement of the season and notice the nuances of the decorative Christmas villages that Kristen Kringles assemble. From the figure eight etched into the skating rink, to the grinchy caroler with the pouty expression, to the glitter in the snow surrounding the train tracks, children can spend hours delighting in Kristen Kringles' meticulously assembled holiday creations. Kristen Kringles who have empty-nest syndrome inquire relentlessly about grandchildren with whom they can share the season.

Thanksgiving: The Countdown *Officially* Begins

Kristen Kringles know that Thanksgiving is merely the opening act to the main event. Many are tempted to pull out the Christmas music during Thanksgiving dinner but know that it's too early to waste it. They settle instead for a television tuned to the Macy's Thanksgiving Day Parade, often getting a chill during the finale when Santa rolls down Broadway. Less patient Kristen Kringles have been known to greet trick-or-treaters at the door wearing elf costumes.

The day after Thanksgiving, Kristen Kringles are nothing less than giddy. Rolling out of bed early, they rush to the stores. Nothing's more energizing than taking part in the hustle and bustle of the holiday. As Kristen Kringles attest, "It makes you feel alive!" Many begin wearing ornament earrings, holiday sweaters, and tinsel in their hair and announce to family and friends that it's "crunch time for the elves." As the twenty-fifth draws nearer they stop saying hello and goodbye and begin picking up the phone saying "Merry Christmas" instead.

Christmas Records: What Does Her Favorite Say About Her Personality?

THE CHRISTMAS RECORD	WHO LIKES IT?
A Charlie Brown Christmas	The connoisseur Kristen Kringle
Elvis or Ella Fitzgerald	The hip Kristen Kringle
Burl Ives, Dean Martin, or Bing Crosby	The cocktail hour Kristen Kringle
Jim Nabors or Perry Como	The clean-living Kristen Kringle
John Tesh or Michael Bolton	The horny Kristen Kringle
Bach/Handel	The NPR-loving Kristen Kringle
Johnny Mathis	The earnest Kristen Kringle
Time-Life: Christmas Memory	The decrepit Kristen Kringle
Alvin and the Chipmunks	The slightly retarded Kristen Kringle
Dixie Chicks	The fully retarded Kristen Kringle

Buying Gifts

Not surprisingly, Kristen Kringles have much longer gift lists than the average person and insist upon shopping for the neighbors, the mailman, and even that friendly cashier at the Safeway whose skin gets so oily. Knowing what to buy people can be tricky, so to make things simpler, many Kristen Kringles start collections for people. They know that if you begin buying decorative salt shakers for Rusty and Pez dispensers for Mike, then next year's gifts will be a cinch. Others whip up a batch of their world-famous Rudolph cookies to give to everyone on their list. Traditionalists prefer giving out holiday standards like Whitman's Samplers and Pepperidge Farm cheese baskets. Kristen Kringles who work decorate their desks with Christmas lights and snow globes, bringing the joy of the season to everyone as their gift.

XenoSantaPhobia

More zealous Kristen Kringles sometimes suffer from XenoSantaPhobia, a disorder that causes them to lash out at people who fail to share their passion for Christmas. XenoSantaPhobia sufferers become enraged by movies that portray Santa Claus as a dishonest drunk. They question the parenting skills of people who don't purchase *real* Christmas trees for their children. Other XenoSantaPhobia sufferers have trouble trusting people who celebrate Hanukkah or Kwanzaa instead of Christmas. *Do they have something against mistletoe and fun*? they wonder. When asked to compare different holidays, many get defensive, saying things like "Thanksgiving is nice but on Christmas you get a meal *and* presents."

The Most Wonderful Time of the Year

When Christmas Eve arrives, Kristen Kringles turn up "Little Drummer Boy" an extra notch and really crank it out. They plug in the mechanical Mr. and Mrs. Claus figures with the robotic arms (although they sometimes frighten the children). They put on Santa hats and curl yards of ribbon with scissors. If there are any extra bows after the gift wrapping is complete, they attach them to their pets' collars. Others make jokes that reference their favorite Christmas movie: "I'm getting my mother-in-law a Red Ryder BB gun, hopefully she won't shoot her eye out."

All Kristen Kringles enjoy making their own traditions out of the simple things: "We gave the cat half a can of *Starkist* tuna last year on Christmas Eve, so make sure you pick up her *traditional* brand, Stanley!" Neglecting the slightest of traditions is the largest of taboos.

When evening comes, Kristen Kringles drive the family around the neighborhood to see the Christmas lights. They keep their fingers crossed that no

The *Other* Sexuals, Part 1

MULTIPLEXUALS (Idio Rank: 5.1)

People who become obsessed with the movie stars they see on the screen at the local multiplex. After seeing the flavor of the month interviewed by Leeza Gibbons, they develop crushes until someone with a fresher look appears on the cover of *Entertainment Weekly*.

INVERSEXUALS (Idio Rank: 6.6)

Men who secure the upper hand in their relationships by refusing to sleep with the women they date. They invert the traditional courting rules by turning women down for sex in order to gain power. Inversexuals usually thwart their lovers' advances by trying to appear damaged or mysteriously aloof.

RETROSEXUALS (Idio Rank: 6.8)

Men with traditional worldviews who decorate their homes with dartboards, brag about hating sushi, and only upgrade their wardrobes when they collect the designated number of Camel Miles for a T-shirt. Traditionally, Retrosexuals have been referred to as frat boys, guidos, meatheads, or sometimes simply as dumbasses.

HYDROSEXUALS (Idio Rank: 8)

Men who are too obsessed with smoking killer hydro weed to be interested in dating. They hang up centerfolds torn form *High Times* magazine on their walls and drool longingly over the crystals, buds, and skunk nugs. It makes them really hot when the bud of the month has red hair.

FLEXISEXUALS (Idio Rank: 5.9)

Straight men who flirt with gay people to secure attention, a job, or a larger tip. If you're not flexible, they attest, women and gays will grab *all* the sugar daddies. Similar to the Heteroflexible, people who are overly bisexual-curious.

FABIOSEXUALS (Idio Rank: 3.9)

Suburban women who have *really* bad taste in men. They base their standard of beauty on pop-culture prototypes like Bob Goen, David Hasselhoff, Michael Bolton, Bill Clinton, and every mustachioed cast member of *As the World Turns*.

one on their block bought the same life-sized reindeer set at Wal-Mart. Others become panicked if they can't locate their copy of *A Miracle on 34th Street*, worrying that Christmas could be ruined should the traditional viewing be neglected.

At ten o'clock, regardless of the age of their children, all Kristen Kringles exclaim, "Better get to sleep, bucko, I hear sleigh bells." This is one of life's great joys. Kristen Kringles get little sleep themselves but enjoy munching on the cookies they left out for Santa. At the strike of midnight, the hallucinatory magic of Christmas has finally arrived and they get all tingly knowing that the big day is here.

Post-Season Distress Disorder

Since all Kristen Kringles feel like the wind has been knocked out of them after the holidays, those with weaker constitutions can become depressed. They find themselves in debt when the bills arrive from their Christmas spending sprees, and many have been known to begin adding extra shots of rum to their leftover eggnog to suppress the pain. Others feel tired and absentminded, shocked to discover they can't recall the name of the reindeer that comes after Prancer.

The Dark Side

Sometimes the sugar-plum exterior of the Kristen Kringle can be deceiving. Similar to the way alcoholics use booze to suppress their unhappiness, many Kristen Kringles hide from the pain of life behind the protection of Santa's steadfast joy. Kristen Kringles who become *too* obsessed with Christmas cut themselves off from friends and family, lose touch with reality, or worse, forget that the true meaning of Christmas comes in the giving.

Some Kristen Kringles have severed relationships with their fathers and turn to Santa to fill the void. Other Kristen Kringles have dysfunctional or unful-filling relationships with their husbands and begin looking to Santa to help them raise the children. "Wait until your father gets home" is often replaced as a disciplinary deterrent by the equally useful "You know Santa is ALWAYS watching." Other Kristen Kringles forget that Santa is make-believe and develop sexual fantasies: "Well, he's certainly good at making toys, so he must be good with his hands."

20 | Ammosexuals

IN BRIEF: Ammosexuals are men with latent testosterone who overcompensate for their less than rugged upbringings by striving to be manly. They're obsessed with being macho. ("Ammo" is an abbreviation for ammunition.)

GENDER: Male

POPULATION SIZE: Moderately rare

HABITAT: Shooting ranges, bars with a good solid arm-wrestling table

HOBBIES: Tying fishing lures, paintball, raising German shepherds, drinking George Dickel, eating ribs, revving up the chainsaw

IDIO RANK: 8.3

Overview

Over the past few years, the media has been obsessed with metrosexuals. In case you've missed out on the exhaustive coverage, a metrosexual is a straight man who enjoys having a manicure, has a taste for sushi, watches *Will & Grace*, and wears expensive leather footwear.

Curiously, a just as recognizable type of heterosexual male known as the Ammosexual has been all but ignored. Ammosexuals are adult males who become obsessed with hunting, motorcycles, firecrackers, extreme sports, and grilling to overcompensate for pampered or overly academic childhoods devoid of masculine rites of passage. Ammosexuals take full advantage of all the manly joys life has to offer. They enjoy rooting, skinning, chewing, whittling, and blowing things up all with equal fervor. Firing semiautomatic weapons at squirrels and chipmunks is another popular pastime. Some famous Ammosexuals include Ted Nugent, Hunter S. Thompson, Chuck Norris, Gary Busey, and, of course, Geraldo. Most Ammosexuals have *Kill It and Grill It* bumper stickers.

Common Misconceptions About Ammosexuals:

MISCONCEPTION #1: *AMMOSEXUALS ARE REDNECKS*
Not to be confused with rednecks, homophobes, militiamen, or neo-Nazis, Ammosexuals are generally quite intelligent and worldly. Though most claim to have gone to the school of hard knocks, in reality most attended schools with much higher tuitions than that particular establishment. Unlike rednecks, Ammosexuals think that discrimination of any kind, whether it be against blacks, homosexuals, or Muslims, is simply wrong. It's perfectly acceptable to make fun of hippies, vegetarians, and PETA though.

MISCONCEPTION #2: *AMMOSEXUALS ARE GAY*
Get real. People mistakenly assume Ammosexuals are in the closet because they try too hard to be manly. In reality, they're asexual. Ammosexuals are only attracted to themselves and love standing in front of full-length mirrors growling in pleasure. Many thrust their pelvises while admiring themselves and ask rhetorically, "Do you like it hard, baby? I'll give it to you hard. Uhh . . . ! Uhh . . . ! Uhh!"
Ammosexuals are largely uninterested in women but sleep with them to assert their dominance, notoriously accruing countless partners to further illustrate their manliness. Despite this indifference, Ammosexuals know that making a woman think you're a little off-kilter or scary can be very satisfying, and even hot. Plus, having women around provides opportunities to fight for their honor, a very macho thing to do.

MISCONCEPTION #3: *ALL GRILLMASTERS ARE AMMOSEXUALS*
Not quite. Though barbequing is an important part of their lifestyle, owning a George Foreman grill alone does not make an Ammosexual. The true Ammosexual enjoys a wide array of activities, such as working on cars, martial arts, bungee jumping, ultimate fighting, smoking stogies, and rattlesnake shoots.

Common Reasons Stated for Becoming an Ammosexual

You may have considered becoming an Ammosexual if:

1. You *really* enjoy eating meat off the bone.
2. People made fun of your small, childlike fingers in high school.
3. No matter how much money you make on Wall Street, your friends still refuse to call you "The Viking."
4. You want to be more like The Nuge.
5. Someone gave you this great Digital Whitetail Deer Call with six deer vocalizations including dominant grunt, social grunt, tending grunt, wheeze, fawn distress, and estrus bleat that you want to put to good use.
6. Your parents refused to let you be in the Boy Scouts as a kid.
7. Camouflage long johns complement your eyes.
8. You think family photos look best when posing with wild game.
9. There was a sale on assault weapons at Kmart.
10. You thought owning a gun rack and a mounted 20-point buck might add some edge to your fiction.

They also MUST know how to open a beer bottle with a lighter. Ammosexuals who have the means enjoy piloting helicopters and driving race cars.

MISCONCEPTION #4: *AMMOSEXUALS EAT ONLY MEAT*

That wouldn't be healthy! Ammosexuals enjoy announcing their hatred of vegetables but secretly like greens or broccoli once some gravy is added.

MISCONCEPTION #5: *AMMOSEXUALS ARE CARD-CARRYING NRA MEMBERS AND REPUBLICANS*

This is partially true. Ammosexuals support the NRA and will be the first to tell you that nothing kills the furry-tailed brush possum more efficiently than a Winchester double-gauged semiautomatic rifle. Other weapons can leave the animal squirming in pain. But hit the little furry-tailed critter with thirty-five caps from this bad boy and he's assured a quick, painless, and humane death.

On the other hand, Ammosexuals are rarely Republicans. They're usually Libertarians and wish the government would just leave them alone. After all, stockpiling grenades *on your own goddamn property* is your God-given right as an American.

MISCONCEPTION #6: *AMMOSEXUALS NEVER LIVE IN CITIES*

A great example of an **Urban Ammosexual** is poet Charles Bukowski. Since cities are often limiting when it comes to expressing their manliness (Bukowski spent most of his adult life in Los Angeles), Urban Ammosexuals overcompensate by hanging out in bars, attending a boxing match, or by going to the offtrack betting booth. All the above are worthy substitutions for hunting and fishing.

Note: Since fiction and poetry are inherently girly flights of fancy, Ammosexuals prefer nonfiction or books written by other Ammosexuals such as Hemingway, McCarthy, and the aforementioned Bukowski.

MISCONCEPTION #7: *AMMOSEXUALS HAVE SMALL PENISES*

This is obviously a misconception. Truth be told, Ammosexuals are a fine size, if you factor in width.

Queer Eye for the Ammosexual

Despite their obsession with being uber-males, Ammosexuals share many similarities with culturally aware gays and metrosexuals. In fact, when it comes to fashion, fine cuisine, and interior design, the Ammosexual's attention to detail is unparalleled. Where gay men and metrosexuals strive for a refined or cultured aesthetic, Ammosexuals strive to dine, dress, and decorate the *Manly Way.*

FASHION/BODY

In one word, rugged. Ammosexuals want to present an outdoorsy irresistibility and prefer shopping at L.L. Bean and places that sell snakeskin camouflage shirts that come with a lifetime guarantee. Not getting shot is also an important consideration when selecting a wardrobe, so fluorescent orange is popular in all seasons. Many Ammosexuals accessorize with grenade launchers and bayonets on the ends of their guns.

MUSCLES

Unlike gays and metrosexuals, Ammosexuals never belong to gyms. When asked why, most claim that weights and treadmills are unnatural. Instead, a man should get his exercise chopping wood, trailing game, scaling trees, or by running up and down the driveway holding a carburetor. Truth be told, many have a phobia of gyms and places with public showers given that locker room bully from childhood with the cold, strong hands.

GROOMING

Ammosexuals opt for extremes when selecting the perfect do. Going bald can be very manly, provided you shave your head using a straight razor and no lotion. When asked about their decision to shave it all off, bald Ammosexuals commonly assert concerns about it getting caught in a table saw. Conversely, a longer pony-tailed look can be very macho, provided you never use a blow-dryer or mousse. Wearing a hat or bandanna adds a degree of macho authenticity to both looks.

When making a decision about facial hair, Ammosexuals rarely choose beards since having one can backfire and make you look cuddly. The day-old stubble look is by far the most popular style. Sandpaper chins simply feel the most badass.

FRAGRANCE

Powder, musk, and summer rain deodorants are for pussies. Ammosexuals prefer unscented soaps, shampoos, and deodorants that leave their natural pheromones to float through the air. Some grow accustomed to Nature's Own Brand *Essence of Whitetail Buck Lure* and apply it liberally before that important date.

THE HOME

Ammosexuals are traditionalists and shun homes designed with a contemporary flair. They prefer more classic dwellings filled with wood-paneled walls and plenty of leather furniture.

Ammosexuals always have a warm spot in their hearts for taxidermy and appreciate the simple elegance a deer head or a stuffed falcon can bring to a home. Mounted crossbows and whips are other timeless classics that can bring warmth to *any* room, regardless of size, style, or color. Subtle touches like a strategically placed copy of *Beef Today* magazine on a coffee table can be a nice conversation piece when company arrives.

When it comes to their lawns, decks, and shooting ranges, Ammosexuals spare no expense. Having an ample number of trees in the yard to pee on is essential when choosing their dream home; it's something in which the Ammosexual can take pride. And when it comes to the grill, they refuse to settle for anything less than the one with the removable spit, which can accommodate up to four Cornish game hens.

Ammosexuals are also known for their obsessive cleanliness. They're always sure to pick the chicken bones, spark plugs, and empty magazine clips up off the floor before things get cluttered. Deer blood is always hosed away with meticulous care.

Ammosexual Lite

A subspecies of Ammosexuals known as **Ammosexual Lites** take their pursuit of being manly to a lesser extreme. Instead of hunting and exploding things, they express their manliness by hosting poker night, smoking cigars, dating strippers, and purchasing velvet-topped pool tables in order to ensure regular male bonding time. Some plan elaborate outings for friends where the boys can go to the dog track, drink bourbon, and top it all off with a titty bar finale. Ammosexual Lites often come across as being a little light on their feet, despite their collections of first-edition Bukowskis. They're simply more interested in the details of being rugged than in being rugged itself. When hosting a poker game, for instance, they're careful about selecting the correct music (Robert Johnson, early Elvis), smoking and drinking the right brands of cigarettes and whiskey (Lucky Strikes, Maker's Mark), and choosing the perfect card table (hard, vintage oak). Poker just isn't as much fun, they know, if you're drinking crappy bourbon out of a cheap, lightweight rocks glass.

WEST WINGNUTS (Idio Rank: 4.3)

West WingNuts are a disenfranchised, highly political American people who long for the compassion and honesty of the leaders on NBC's *The West Wing*. Frustrated by the daily news and the political decisions made by the current president, West WingNuts turn to the television show to help them formulate their political opinions. More importantly, they turn to it for comfort. West WingNuts find the sensitive and honest president played by Martin Sheen refreshing and enjoy fantasizing what life would be like if Sheen was to actually hold office. Some place televisions in their bathrooms and take Calgon baths while watching CJ, Josh, and Toby on TV. *West Wing* marathons are the major television event of the year.

21 | Lieberals
(Lee-bur-ohls)

IN BRIEF: Named for conservative Democrat Joe Lieberman, Lieberals are overly PC Democrats who water down their liberal tendencies in order to do what's best for children.

GENDER: Male or female

POPULATION SIZE: Common

HABITAT: Anywhere, but especially the Northeast

FAVORITE BOOKS: Anything by Bill Moyers

FAVORITE MUSIC: Ken Burns's Jazz series box set

IDIO RANK: 3.6

Overview

The process of becoming a tad more conservative with age is a well-documented phenomenon, and the number of Democrats comfortable with the term "family values" is on the rise. In the eighties, formerly liberal baby boomers were often criticized for subscribing to the *Wall Street Journal*, power lunching, buying expensive cars, and becoming Yuppies.

Lieberals are easily distinguished from Yuppies because instead of basing their conservative leanings on fiscal concerns, they shape their worldview on what's best for children. Many Lieberals have kids of their own and use this *child filter* to formulate their decisions on everything from First Amendment issues to taxes to *Survivor*. Unlike Yuppies, who are part of a very specific demographic, Lieberals can be a member of any voting age demographic, as is indicated by the Brown University campus. Regardless, most Lieberals are middle-aged and have families of their own. All Lieberals suspiciously overutilize the word "sensible." More religious Lieberals insist on using the politically correct term for homosexual, "sodomite."

Lieberals generally come from the middle class to upper middle class in notably homogeneous, white neighborhoods. They prefer city life when they're young but move to the suburbs after marrying to ensure that their children are brought up in good public school districts. Many Lieberals enlist their children in private schools where the curriculums include candle making and madrigal singing alongside math and science.

Signs You're a Lieberal, Part 1:

▶ You've traded in your Volkswagen for a Volvo or a Saab.
▶ You own a copy of Tipper Gore's *Joined at the Heart: The Transformation of the American Family*.
▶ You limit your children to a maximum of two hours of television per week.
▶ You sometimes wonder why no one at work wants to discuss *Prairie Home Companion* around the water cooler with you on Mondays.
▶ You think we should end tax cuts in favor of more liberal tax claims.
▶ You're active in the church or synagogue but wish they would use gender-neutral pronouns when reading from the religious texts.
▶ You canceled your subscription to *Harper's* in favor of *Newsweek*.

The First Amendment

When it comes to the idea of freedom of speech, Lieberals are its strongest defenders, provided the individuals pushing the boundaries agree to show some doggone respect for others. Lieberals recognize the difference between expressing yourself and being a creep. They understand that there's no place for smut like *Maxim*, shoot-'em-up movies, Howard Stern, or nipples in a civilized society. Similarly, Lieberals believe that rap lyrics have infected today's family like the plague. Kids need to listen to music that has a positive message. Nevertheless, Lieberals universally endorse Will Smith as a good role model for children.

The Problem with Kids These Days

As any good Lieberal will attest, there's nothing wrong with today's youth. The problem lies with the lack of moral guidance. Families should spend less time watching the idiot box and more time actively seeking out constructive and creative activities. Reading aloud from a children's classic like *The Wind in the Willows* is a nice alternative to television. Establishing an Iron Kid night where the children are encouraged to experiment cooking new dishes can be a blast. Or how about having a papier-mâché sculpture contest where everyone wins? Turning the television off in favor of activities such as these instills confidence in children. It helps them to make the right decisions about drugs and sex. And when you think about it, most of what you find on TV is garbage anyway, with the exception of PBS. Many Lieberals take breaks from their televisions for months on end after getting angry at negativity and violence on the network news. *Why can't they run positive stories?* they wonder.

Violence and Staying "With It"

In contrast to Republicans, who consider the pornography industry to be society's largest moral offender, Lieberals believe that pornography takes a backseat to violence. Shoot-'em-up video games and movies with guns in them desensitize youth to violence and are the primary reason our schools have become unsafe. Columbine probably would not have happened had the record labels put their foot down and refused to publish violent lyrics by Marilyn Manson. And don't even get them started on BB guns, parents who spank, or dodgeball.

Lieberals all have a subscription to the Sunday *New York Times* and quote religiously from it in conversation, regardless of where they live. They tend to listen to NPR obsessively and feel the only decent reality show is *This American Life*. Years of listening to public radio often affects their speech patterns, conditioning them to overenunciate, as if they were reading a book to children. This comes in handy since they love reading books to children.

Lieberals always vote for Democrats and would never own guns, endorse school vouchers, watch a boxing match, shop at Wal-Mart, or worse, catch a lightning bug and not let it go. Always supporters of the arts, Lieberals fight tooth and nail to secure government funding for institutions that show cutting-edge art like Chagall and Picasso. When it comes to the polarizing abortion issue, Lieberals support a woman's right to choose but have to draw the line when it comes to partial birth abortions. After all, they don't even know what the term "partial birth abortion" means.

To let you know they're still "with it," many male Lieberals grow goatees and keep their hair a tad longer. Female Lieberals often wear tennis shoes to the office or allow their husbands to cook dinner one night a month to illustrate that they're feminists.

RU-PUBLICANS (Idio Rank: 8.2)

If you commonly say "Why don't we just bomb the bastards?" then change the subject to what a hot piece of ass Britney Spears is, chances are strong that you're a Ru-publican. Named for the conservative Fox Media owner, *Ru*pert Murdoch, Ru-publicans are an increasingly common breed of conservative who like their family values peppered with a little kinkiness. The Murdoch media staples Fox News, *New York Post*, and the *Sun* all have a trademark gumbo of "family" values spiced up with celebrity gossip. After all, those latte-drinking, tax-raising, gay-marriage-promoting liberals in Hollywood may be disgraceful, but their celebrity scandals and free-flowing cleavage sure are fun to watch. Not to mention the fact that they help to raise ratings and stock prices.

Most conservatives emphasize the importance of promoting strong family values, so it's not surprising that Ru-publicans share their concerns. Many conservatives feel that in life, God, family, and country should always come first. Ru-publicans, on the other hand, have a different hierarchy altogether. To them, low taxes, missionary-position sex, and a strong military should always come first. Conservatives often turn to religious texts such as the Bible to answer life's tough questions. The Ru-publican's religious text of choice is the IRS Tax Guide.

Ru-publicans commonly mask their conservative biases behind slogans like "No Spin Zone" and "Fair and Balanced." Truth be told, they're very proud of their beliefs and in an ideal world would rather be up front about their conservative leanings. Nevertheless, Ru-publicans know that claiming outright to be a political conservative deeply decreases the odds of getting laid.

Signs You're a Lieberal, Part 2:

▶ You frequently use the terms "sensible," "civil union," "slippery slope," and "people of color."

▶ When hot under the collar, you've been known to refer to someone as a *jerk*.

▶ You endorse equal rights for women but think that Camille Paglia is a little "out there."

▶ You often wonder why Al Sharpton can't be more like Martin Luther King or Booker T. Washington.

▶ You support any war overseas, as long as it's referred to as a peace-keeping mission.

▶ You've given up political activism in favor of boycotting.

▶ Every time you go to 7-Eleven you find yourself mumbling that the lottery is a tax on the poor.

▶ When discussing the welfare system, gay marriage, or affirmative action, you change the subject by saying "Now there's a tricky issue."

▶ You're an advocate of social diversity in your community and have that nice black couple, the Jenkins, over for dinner once a month.

▶ When making a fist, you place your thumb on top of your index finger.

22 | Silver Surfers

IN BRIEF: Senior citizens who go through a second puberty after retiring, also known as Geriatric Sexcats

GENDER: Male or female

POPULATION SIZE: Moderately common

HABITAT: On silk sheets, the bathroom at Denny's

FAVORITE READING: *Penthouse* Forum, *Guidepost* Forum

IDIO RANK: 5.9

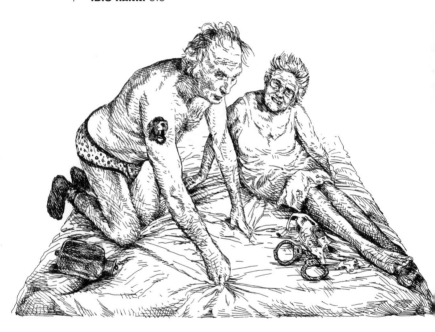

Overview

In this country, senior citizens never get the respect they deserve. People who are in their golden years are, more often than not, treated in very demeaning ways. People automatically assume that mental alertness, energy level, and sex drive all decline after sixty. Truth be told, as you get older you get more experienced and wise. Especially in the sack. Retired life opens up people's schedules, leaving more time to score some booty. In the age of Viagra that we've entered, senior citizens aren't "frisky." They're horny. Just like everybody else. Let's face it, if Bob Dole can get some action, lots of older people must be having sex.

As baby boomers prepare to retire, sex has become even more accepted as normal and natural for those of advanced years. The next time you're behind a senior couple driving slowly in the fast lane, it could be they're driving slowly because they're doing it.

The Silver Years

Everybody has run into an elderly couple who is outspoken about their sexual appetite, but Silver Surfers take that to a different level altogether. They are insatiable. Silver Surfers have the libidos of twenty-year-olds and stock their homes with tantric sex guides, leopard-skin lingerie, slinky leotards, revealing briefs, and Advanced Warming Power BenGay.

Contrary to popular belief, not all Silver Surfers live in Miami. They're everywhere. Many are widows or widowers who experience a sexual awakening with a new partner. Some simply grow closer to their spouses over the years and feel their sexual desire for them become more fervent.

Others discover staying sexually active makes them feel younger and decide it's never too late to experiment. A lot. After all, if having your teeth in a glass kills the mood, just turn the lights out. Silver Surfers who are single sometimes spend time at Linens 'n Things to meet hot geriatric chicks.

The Old and the Beautiful

Many seniors surgically enhance themselves or get Botox injections to prolong the illusion of youth. Silver Surfers, on the other hand, would rather not bother. They know that being old can be beautiful and that the early-bird special doesn't have to refer to a four o'clock dinner at Cracker Barrel. As all Silver Surfers will attest, sex after sixty can be very fulfilling. After menopause, women don't have to worry about birth control. Hickeys are easily explained away as age spots. Arthritic ice packs and heating pads make great sex toys.

Younger friends and family commonly worry about the health of the Silver Surfers they know, warning them that too much sex could lead to heart attacks. Silver Surfers know that going out that way would be pretty fucking cool. Life is simply too short to let a pacemaker, an enlarged prostate, or a case of angina get in the way of some mind-blowing lovin'.

Favorite Silver Surfer Pickup Lines, Part 1:

▶ Your heating pad or mine?
▶ I may be old, but I don't have that old person smell yet.
▶ I live on the *first* floor.
▶ What's a nice girl like you doing on an oxygen respirator?
▶ So where were *you* when Kennedy was shot?

- I like what gravity has done to those hips of yours.
- I've got the first season of *Murder, She Wrote* on DVD.
- Anyone ever told you that you look like Lady Bird Johnson?
- So, baby, what HMO plan do you use?
- (For bald Silver Surfers only) In case you're wondering, the drapes *do* match the carpet.
- Ever done it with a shriner?

   Note: *Silver Surfers who are trying to court younger lovers rarely have much success with the lines "Last time I saw you, you were this tall" or "Wanna sit on my lap?"*

Silver Surfer Tips to Making it SIZZLE

Silver Surfers are more forthright about their sexuality than most seniors. They're secure with their bodies and know that having a healthy sex life makes you feel better about yourself. Plus, it's great exercise. We polled several Silver Surfers to find what they do to fan the flames. Here's what we found.

EXPERIMENT WITH NEW THINGS

Try new positions like the wheelbarrow, the scissors, or the granddaddy long-legs. And don't be afraid to experiment with new positions using his walker. Despite its name, that's not the only thing it's good for! Try having phone sex or take a class that teaches you how to use e-mail so you can shower your lover's in-box with sweet nothings. Some Silver Surfers enjoy bringing food into the bedroom. Feed you lover grapes, chocolates, and rice cakes sprinkled with Mrs. Dash. From time to time, let your partner have some ice cream after nine o'clock, even if the doctor said he/she shouldn't.

   Remember that bedroom dynamics do change with age. For instance, when talking seductively, choosing an appropriate pet name for an older lover is important. No one wants to hear, "Come here, Granny, I'm ready for some lovin'." This can, in fact, break the mood.

BE SPONTANEOUS, VARIETY IS THE SPICE OF LIFE

Spend an afternoon at a hot XXX theater with your senior citizen's gold pass followed by a late dinner at 4:30 P.M. Take some of *his* pills. Go for a skinny-dip in the pond behind the nursing home. And don't be fooled into thinking sex can only happen in the bedroom. Mix things up a bit. Do it in different places in the house, like the kitchen, the living room, or by the mothballs in the attic. Experiment with making love at different times each day. Instead of just having routine sex in the evening after *Touched by an Angel*, have mind-blowing sex in the afternoon just before pinochle.

THE RIGHT MUSIC

To get in the mood, put on some hot music like "Ghost Riders in the Sky" by the Sons of the Pioneers. Time-Life collections that feature hits by Anne Murray, Tony Orlando, or Benny Goodman always put the senior libido into fifth gear. When the mood is right, pop on "Tie a Yellow Ribbon Round the Ole Oak Tree." It's a sensual classic that always turns the heat WAY up.

MULTIPLE PARTNERS

Some Silver Surfers enjoy the swinger's life by inviting new people into the bedroom. The dynamic of a new person can be a thrill, but Silver Surfers should avoid suggesting ménages with their convalescent nurses.

EXPERIENCE SENSUALITY

The key to great sex is focusing on what makes one another feel good. Turn off your hearing aid so that you can really concentrate on what makes your partner feel good. Younger couples often rub oil on one another's bodies, but as you age you may find that low-salt margarine works just as well, especially for cardiac patients who enjoy kissing you all over. Sometimes nothing is a bigger turn-on than simply spending time together. Put some candles in the bathroom and take a bath together. Or read the *Reader's Digest* or *TV Guide* aloud together. Nothing is hotter.

Favorite Silver Surfer Pickup Lines, Part 2:

▶ Every tried a 79?

▶ Is it my dementia talking or are you superhot?

▶ Is that a hot flash or are you just happy to see me?

▶ I just finished estrogen replacement therapy.

▶ Once you go flaccid, you never go back.

▶ Didn't we meet at the army/navy mixer after storming the beaches of Normandy?

▶ That polyester pantsuit matches your eyes.

▶ These bones may be brittle, but I could diddle your skittle.

▶ I have the cholesterol of a twenty-five-year-old.

▶ That hairstyle looks just as good now as it did in 1962.

▶ My nursing home has HBO.

▶ My Viagra will be kicking in in about five minutes.

▶ Ever done it with a mason?

THE LURE (Idio Rank: 8.1)

Anyone who is twenty-one years old in this country immediately has an advantage over those who are younger. Namely, they can legally buy beer. People who are a bit socially stunted sometimes even use this to their advantage. Lures are older men who buy beer for high school kids so they can party with them. Sometimes they invite themselves to social events by saying "Know of any ragers going on this weekend? Let me know and I'll pick up some beers for us." Others find that a great way to meet people is to introduce themselves to high school chicks at the mall, saying "You know, Shop 'n Save has Molson bottles on sale this week." Other Lures invite their younger sibling's friends over to their apartments on the weekends to drink beer and play video games. They know that setting an example for promising youngsters can be fulfilling and rewarding.

23 | Sportriots

(Sport-tree-uts)

IN BRIEF: People who think soccer is un-American and/or not masculine

GENDER: Male

POPULATION SIZE: Moderately common

HABITAT: Football stadiums, The Mike Ditka Cultural Museum

HOBBIES: Being a good American, wife beating, eating Vienna sausages out of the can

FAVORITE BOOK: *Guffaws with Bradshaw: The Story of an American Hero*

IDIO RANK: 8.7

Overview

Anyone who's ever played soccer knows that it's a high-intensity game. It's among the fastest paced sports one can play and requires not only strength but endurance, skill, and flexibility. Many argue that soccer is more physically intense than football or basketball. The sport even has a history filled with violence. Legend has it that in the first soccer game ever played in England no ball was used, but the head of a Danish prince who had been defeated in battle.

Nevertheless, a common type of sports fan known as the Sportriot considers the game to be unmanly. Real sports have contact, they claim. Football is a man's sport. Basketball is a man's sport. Boxing is a man's sport. And, of course, sitting in front of the TV eating a meat-lover's pizza with a bag of chips while watching any of the above is manly too.

Sportriots can prove that soccer is gay with two words: exposed legs. Sure, basketball players wear shorts too, but they don't run around grassy fields staring at each other's hairy legs. Plus, basketball players had the sense to get rid of short shorts in the seventies. Further proof is the fact that the American soccer season begins in the spring, that "faggy" time of the year when flowers and robins come out and poets begin to write sonnets. The average Sportriot envisions the locker room after a soccer match as being much like the set of a gay porn film. They'd rather their sons be gay than play soccer. Actually, playing soccer and being gay are essentially the same thing to them.

The History of the Sportriot

This soccer-loathing species began to flourish during the McCarthy era. Renowned xenophobes, they believe that not only is soccer unmanly, it's un-American. The enormous appeal of the sport overseas makes them even more suspicious. The World Cup is watched by billions of people, so clearly there must be some serious subliminal communist brainwashing going on since it's so boring. Worst of all, they worry that soccer could one day replace football in popularity. The thought of Hank Williams Jr. singing "Are you ready for some soccer?" is an apocalyptic vision to them.

Most Sportriots played football in high school and remain friends with someone who still goes by the nickname "Hoss." They look up to Mike Ditka, John Madden, Michael "Refrigerator" Perry, and other sports stars with mayonnaise-filled bodies. Sportriots from the older generation sometimes claim to have spotted soccer balls when they were storming the beaches of Normandy.

The Worldview of the Sportriot

People have been claiming for years that soccer is catching on in America. They're wrong. Most Americans still prefer watching football, baseball, and NASCAR. Sportriots are quick to point this out whenever someone mentions the stronghold soccer has gained in American society. On the other hand, the narrow-minded worldview of the Sportriot is absolutely on the rise. Like a disease-causing gene, this hatred of the game is often passed from one generation to the next, preventing the acceptance of soccer as a real sport. To better understand the perplexing mind-set of the Sportriot, we talked to one to document his controversial beliefs firsthand:

A Sportriot Cites Why Soccer Is Un-American:

▶ There are too many ties. Americans kick ass. We don't settle for ties.
▶ Osama bin Laden used to play soccer at those al-Quaeda training camps, you know.
▶ Like rap, soccer causes violence. Just look at those hooligans fighting every year at the big games.

- I don't buy imported cars and I don't play imported sports.
- You always hear it's the world's favorite spectator sport, but that's because the press is run by New York City liberals who would love to see our American traditions like NASCAR and Monday Night Football taken away.
- What the heck is nil? We call it zero over here, buddy. What's next, the metric system? Socialism? Anarchy?
- Those soccer wackos have been trying to steal the name "football" from us for years.
- Unlike most sports, which require costly gear (pads, baskets, cars), soccer can be played by anyone. All you need is a ball. Sounds a little bit like communism, don'tcha think?
- If soccer catches on here, then people will want to internationalize the NFL too. There's no way my Packers are gonna play some Swedish team.
- Americans suck at soccer. France is good at it. Need I say more?

A Sportriot Cites Why Soccer Is Gay:

- Real men tackle. Girls kick.
- Soccer players have gay haircuts and names like Pelé and Romanio that sound more like fashion designers.
- There's not enough scoring, and as anyone who watched *Porky's I, II,* and *III* can tell you, being a man is all about scoring.
- Why can't they use their arms? What do they think is going to happen? Like homosexuality, soccer defies the laws of nature.
- Britain is the birthplace of modern soccer. And come on, we all know a lot of the Brits are a little light on their feet, if you know what I mean.
- All the dorks in high school played soccer. They all thought they were so smart. Especially that Michael Belatante kid who you *know* turned out to be gay. Kickball was so much better. And remember dodgeball? Now *that* was a game.
- Those tall socks look like panty hose, and I'll give you three guesses why their players don't need cups.
- The International Football Association Board rule book all but states that soccer is gay:

    "If, when a throw-in is being taken, any of the opposing players dance about or gesticulate in a way calculated to distract or impede the thrower, it shall be deemed ungentlemanly conduct."

Gesticulate? That's definitely gay.

The Other Sexuals, Part 2

KLEPTOSEXUALS (Idio Rank: 8.1)

Women who date rich, successful men to secure free drinks, expensive dinners, and luxury weekends away in the country. They scour bars where drinks cost ten dollars a pop, knowing that affordable bars only attract losers who make the same amount of money as they do. Some Kleptosexuals marry their victims to secure solid divorce settlements.

PERPLEXUALS (Idio Rank: 3.8)

Charismatic people who perplex their friends by consistently choosing dull and/or unattractive partners.

POMOSEXUALS (Idio Rank: 5.9)

Women who like "PoMo" (PostModern) boys who wear tight ironic T-shirts and weigh less than they do.

SALINESEXUALS (Idio Rank: 3.9)

Men who prefer peroxide blondes with fake breasts like Pamela Anderson. Most subscribe to *Stuff* and think that women dig dudes who go au naturel beneath stonewashed jeans.

HAIR GEL KNIGHTS (Idio Rank: 8.8)

Meathead men who believe that chivalry is alive and well and try to impress women by defending their honor. Hair Gel Knights stand when a woman enters the room. They pull out their chairs for them before they sit down. They believe their grail quest is to locate someone who glances at their dates so they can kick his ass.

SHADOWSEXUALS (Idio Rank: 7.1)

Shadowsexuals enjoy being with short women they have to bend down to kiss. The psychological thrill of towering over their partners provides a rush for them. Most are control freaks and inherently want to provide protection for their partners when scary stuff happens, like thunderstorms.

24 | OB/GY-Wiccans
(O-B-G-Y Wik-ins)

IN BRIEF: Middle-aged, obese, Wiccan sex specialists
GENDER: Female
POPULATION SIZE: Moderately rare
HABITAT: Midwest, West Coast, the fishnet stocking aisle at Rite Aid
FAVORITE BOOKS: *The Goth Kama Sutra, Betty Crocker's Cauldron Cookbook*
FAVORITE MUSIC: Pagan Peggy and the "no, we're not Satanists" choir
IDIO RANK: 7.3

Overview

OB/GY-Wiccans are an unusual breed of sex therapists, counselors, and libidinous authors. Generally into Goth as teens (see section on Food Court Druids), OB/GY-Wiccans develop a fondness for all things black (nail polish, dresses, fishnet stockings) and carry this preference with them into adulthood. As their vibrant sexual curiosity begins to ripen with age, they become especially interested in enhancing their sex lives with ancient spiritual truth and begin cultivating knowledge in a grab bag of New Age subjects including astrology, tantric sex, the crop circles, Kama Sutra, libido-stimulating creams and herbs, and of course Wicca and bonbons.

The Entrepreneur

OB/GY-Wiccans feel out of place in the uptight world of corporate America and uniformly refuse to work in environments that prohibit the burning of incense or pan flute music. Instead, OB/GY-Wiccans choose a career within the lucrative sex and/or New Age industries.

During their twenties, OB/GY-Wiccans become quite learned in New Age spirituality and often take jobs at crystal shops and occult bookstores, where they can deepen their knowledge. Others find work in adult bookstores and massage parlors, even though they'd rather be strippers.

Upon reaching their full Earth Mother girth in their thirties, many OB/GY-Wiccans begin writing and self-publishing provocative sexual guidebooks. Others become sex gurus and open up their houses to strangers by advertising themselves as sex counselors on the bulletin board at ShopRite. To illustrate that women of any size can be beautiful, they wear lacy black slip dresses that show off lots of cleavage. Many OB/GY-Wiccans have tongue, belly button, and clitoral piercings and buy large ornate rings for every finger to accentuate their allure.

Their clients, fans, and readers consist of sexually liberated adults who have become tired of the watered-down teachings of Dr. Phil and desire candid sexual instruction. OB/GY-Wiccans help their clients, fans, and readership by explaining the difference between sexuality and sensuality and by integrating spirituality into the bedroom. Many pick up some extra cash on the side by selling rabbit-fur massage mits and sex toys emblazoned with dragon imagery. The ultimate goal of the OB/GY-Wiccan is to appear on HBO's *Real Sex* show or to secure a forum for her teachings on a local radio station or public access television station.

Some Popular Book Titles Published by OB/GY-Wiccans

- ▶ *No Broomstick Required: The Official Guide to Dating, Seducing, and Loving Pagans*
- ▶ *Unleashing the Hidden Sex Goddess (Beneath Those Chins)*
- ▶ *The Tao of Pussy*
- ▶ *S.A.T.A.N.—Sexually Advanced Tempestuous And Normal*
- ▶ *Integrating Dungeon & Dragons Dice into a Healthy Sex Life*
- ▶ *Raising a Family in the Nude*
- ▶ *Consciousness, Eros, Chocolate Pudding*
- ▶ *In Nomine Babalon: Sacred Whoredom in Thelemic Context*
- ▶ *Dominatrix Dungeon Feng Shui*
- ▶ *Magick Tits*

A Classic Erotic Poem by an OB/GY-Wiccan

Open thine mind's eye
For the Fey Folk are wild
And the visit of the Faerie on a whip-poor-will's wisp
Is telling and can teach you of Venus's bliss
Onward, make haste, give Hecate her due
Her forests are untamed
Like the Passion between you

Faire Lady, faire Man
And ye partners of hand
Be like the Faeries of the field
Who run with the Wolf
Streams of delight you shall share
The moon o'erhead, beWitches the air

Lighteth the Eternal Candelabra
On the winged precipice of carnal tryst
Be Free, mystical, libidinous.
Faire Lady, faire Man
And ye partners of hand
Become
Celestial
Dancers.

Better Homes and Dungeons

OB/GY-Wiccans understand the importance of family but prefer the single life and rarely marry. Nevertheless, they love kids and tend to adopt a few of their own or find a lover who will agree to join them on the sex swing to help them along in the process.

OB/GY-Wiccans enjoy teaching their children about sex at an early age. They often walk around the house in the nude to illustrate that they're comfortable with their bodies. All OB/GY-Wiccans encourage safe sexual exploration for their children. Children of OB/GY-Wiccans tend to conform to their mothers' dress styles by wearing black nail polish and black clothing exclusively. But they have occasionally been known to rebel against their mothers' sexual openness by becoming withdrawn, starting fights in mosh pits, or by killing five local children to represent all five points of the pentagram.

The dawn of the Internet has helped foster an enormous growth in the OB/GY-Wiccan community. Now, with the click of a mouse, OB/GY-Wiccans can easily publish their sexual tomes and attach the title "Dr." to their names without fear of legal repercussions. Needless to say, the use of particularly bad clip art featuring wizards, wolves, and unicorns has also surged.

Johanna Pieterman

Artists throughout the ages have always relied on muses to inspire their creative process. Some have found inspiration in the beautiful countryside of Spain or France. Others have been roused by the warm caress of a lover. Some have even found encouragement in the work of another artist.

Johanna Pieterman is an artist, illustrator, and portraitist who was born in the Netherlands in 1966. She cites her inspirations as being "nature and all the wonderful creatures of Mother Earth . . . her faeries, animals, flowers, and the vast Universe with its planets, its stars, and all the different realms where beauty lives."

Johanna Pieterman also has a much more compelling muse: the popular Fleetwood Mac singer Stevie Nicks. Johanna began drawing the "rock-and-roll ballerina" when she was sixteen. She was doing homework in her room when she first heard "Edge of Seventeen." She was on the edge of seventeen herself, and when she heard Stevie's distinctive croon, her "books flew through the air." Clearly, Stevie was speaking to her personally. Johanna began collecting Fleetwood Mac records and drawing Stevie soon after.

Johanna uses colored pencils, as well as metallic ink, gold leafing, and watercolors in her work. She has provided illustrations for two Stevie Nicks books, *Rock's Mystical Lady* and *Lady of the Stars.*

Since Stevie's favorite instrument is the tambourine, Johanna often creates customized Stevie tambourines that can be ordered on her Web site. She also does wonderful portraits of people posing with Stevie. Send her a check and a

A Stevie Nicks portrait by Johanna Pieterman

photo of yourself and you can be immortalized with the rock-and-roll diva your-self. Bookmarks, stationery, and illustrations of Stevie with wolves and crystal balls are available as well.

Visit her online at www.johannas-art.com.

Oxymorons,
Peculiar Hybrids,
and
Fish Out of Water

Jumbo Shrimp. Virtual Reality. Jews for Jesus. Bestselling author James Patterson. Microsoft Works. Wal-Mart health plan. Limp Bizkit's greatest hits. The Dodge Ram. Some things in life just don't seem to fit.

Everybody has felt out of place at one time or another. Like being the only person at a formal dinner wearing sneakers. Or being the only one to arrive at a peace rally in a Hummer. Some go through life trying to set themselves apart from the status quo, while others are simply unaware that they don't quite fit in. In part 5 of this book, we will discuss Idio Types who distinguish themselves (whether consciously or unconsciously) by living their lives out of step with others. They are the Oxymorons, the Peculiar Hybrids, and the Fish Out of Water.

This image indicates that more thorough research on this particular Idio Type is pending.

25 | Asphalt Rangers

(a.k.a. Urban Backpackers)

IN BRIEF: Activists protesting the fashion-obsessed decadence of city life by wearing backpacking gear

GENDER: Male or female

POPULATION SIZE: Moderately common

HABITAT: Major urban centers, Green Party rallies, co-op markets, Karen's Carob Counter

HOBBIES: Knitting, collecting bungee cords, applying moleskin to a lover's feet

FAVORITE BOOKS: *Our Bodies, Ourselves; L.L. Bean catalog; Genetically Engineer This: A Supermarket Horror Story*

IDIO RANK: 3.9

Overview

Walk ten city blocks in any major metropolitan area in the United States and you're sure to encounter an Asphalt Ranger. Easily identified by their enormous L.L. Bean backpacks, hiking boots, parkas, and, occasionally, walking sticks, Asphalt Rangers have become an inevitable part of the social fabric found in cities ranging from New York to Atlanta to San Francisco. If you're riding the subway and the person next to you whips out a canteen, chances are you are in the presence of an Asphalt Ranger.

Asphalt Rangers usually migrate to the city from rural and scenic locales such as Maine, Colorado, Oregon, and Vermont. Their childhoods are spent playing in the woods, swinging in hemp hammocks, and running barefoot on gravel to determine which of their peers has the toughest feet. They flock to large cities after graduating from college (against their better judgment) to secure jobs in the nonprofits. Popular colleges for Asphalt Rangers include Reed, Evergreen, and any private institution where drinking from a Styrofoam cup warrants irreparable social ostracism.

The Asphalt Rangers' Ethos

Often confused with hippies, given their *Back to Eden* sensibilities, Asphalt Rangers are nonetheless a very different breed of people who identify with hippies only on very saccharine levels. Like hippies, they are environmentally conscious and advocates of social reform, but Urban Backpackers tend to be notably more ambitious and healthy than hippies. They rarely do drugs or drink to excess, but do go a little overboard on the trail mix.

The Asphalt Rangers' Five Stages of Acceptance

1. Denial—Upon relocating to the city, Asphalt Rangers enter into a hazy state of disbelief, refusing to deal with the stress of being uprooted. Many complain of feeling numb or tingly. Others resort to writing bleak poetry entries about machines, assembly lines, and ant colonies.

2. Anger—At this stage, Asphalt Rangers often become frustrated by the cultural differences they encounter in the city. Many lash out by tossing glass and metal containers into the garbage with the nonrecyclables. Commonly, Asphalt Rangers will become enraged by the crowds they encounter on the sidewalk and forcefully brush up against pedestrians with their gear. Some even get angry at God, beseeching him for allowing so many Starbucks to exist. More radical Asphalt Rangers have even been known to let a piece of trash fall from their hands on the street *and leave it there*.

3. Bargaining—During the bargaining stage, Asphalt Rangers try to temper their trauma with misplaced hope and fantasizing. They convince themselves that weekend retreats to more scenic locales will help compensate for the pain they experience during the week. *If I stick to this city life thing for a year or so, I will be rewarded with job opportunities allowing me to work anywhere I want, perhaps upstate on a farm.* Others begin wearing designer clothing, drinking cosmos, and hanging out in trendy clubs hoping to fit in. Urban Backpackers who choose the latter route are doomed to failure when they commit social faux pas such as pulling out a Velcro wallet at a trendy French bistro.

4. Depression—During this stage, many Asphalt Rangers become withdrawn and deal with their anger by knitting bulky wool sweaters or practicing melancholy songs on a recorder. Some unpack their old camping gear and begin setting up tents inside their apartments. Insomnia is a common problem during this phase, and Asphalt Rangers often purchase tapes featuring the sounds of waterfalls to help them sleep. Many stop walking altogether and put on a few pounds eating Ben & Jerry's, despite the fact that the company owners sold out.

5. Acceptance—Asphalt Rangers achieve the stage of acceptance by immersing themselves in their work and embracing their new environments as home. Hopeful that there is light (and preferably grass) at the end of the tunnel, they begin acquainting themselves with local recycling policies, making friends with neighbors and coworkers, walking around the neighborhood to pick up trash, and finding moments of contentment by visiting a local park where a bald eagle was recently spotted. Females show a ritualistic display of conformance by shaving their legs and armpits. Males begin combing their beards. Most trade in their hiking boots for New Balance sneakers, a ritual that is commonly emblematic of healing and acceptance.

Blessed Are the Frugal

Asphalt Rangers all agree that decadence and waste are at the root of most social problems in contemporary society. In response to these concerns, they tend to be very frugal and practical. They prefer athletic bras to Victoria's Secret lingerie. Hiking boots to sneakers. Denim to silk. And quality and durability are always more important than being fashionable. All Asphalt Rangers have a favorite pair of worn denim jeans and sometimes give them nicknames like "Ole '98" or "The Road Warriors."

Asphalt Rangers' apartments are filled with air mattresses, Tom Robbins paperbacks, whittling knifes, Audubon Society membership plaques, and a closet for parkas and tents. A minimal approach to decorating works well for them, given the lower wages nonprofit employees typically receive. More fortunate Asphalt Rangers, who are blessed by the unexpected visit of a cricket in their homes, delight in the comfort of its chirping as day moves into night.

Not surprisingly, their penchant for being practical is also represented in their diets. Asphalt Rangers grow up eating healthy foods grown locally. Big fans of the outdoor barbeque, Asphalt Rangers often feel torn about vegetarianism due to their fondness for grilling. Their parents' prohibition of sugar and unhealthy snacks leads many to feign diabetes later in life to explain their compulsion to snack on Snickers, Twinkies, and other unhealthy treats that would otherwise undermine their healthy-living philosophies.

Asphalt Rangers rarely eat out and make a point to stock their backpacks every evening with the next day's breakfast and lunch. They own one solitary Ziploc bag that they use time and time again, rinsing it out after each use. Their tendency to bring their own lunch to work comes in handy since fitting down the narrow aisles of a city deli is next to impossible given the girth of their gear. It should be noted that less savvy Urban Backpackers are sometimes neglectful in cleaning their bags and need to be reminded when remnants of yesterday's lunch begin to spoil.

Thirst, Safety, and Lots of Walking

Asphalt Rangers prefer walking to work whenever possible and therefore try to avoid sleeping late in the morning. They uniformly despise the global oil industry and protest it by avoiding cars and other gas- and oil-based forms of transit whenever they can. Plus, they enjoy fantasizing that they're on the Appalachian Trail. Many apply bug spray and sunblock to enhance the fantasy. Others incorporate sunrise poetry sessions into their morning routines, feeling inspired by the music of sparrows before the cacophony of city life sets in.

All Asphalt Rangers have an innate fear of thirst and carry a minimum of three water bottles in their backpacks at any given time. This often leads to chronic back pain, stiff knees, and weak ankles, which become problematic for older Asphalt Rangers. Other health problems have been known to arise when Urban Backpackers venture into crime-ridden neighborhoods, where they are often teased by local youth, who call them names such as Ranger Rick or Smokey the Cracker. Many Asphalt Rangers are fans of biking and discover that bike pumps make handy weapons should the need arise.

Though most work in casual environments, on occasion Asphalt Rangers are placed in situations where they must dress formally. At graduations, funerals, and Quaker mass, where more formal attire is mandatory, male Asphalt Rangers voice a subtle fashion protest by wearing seersucker suits or bright polyester ties. Female Urban Backpackers choose baggy dark-colored dresses that look like maternity wear. Their bodies are usually honed and slender from exercise and Clif Bars, but wearing sexy, body-revealing dresses would defy The Code.

In the long run, Asphalt Rangers are rarely cut out for the city life and begin longing for more scenic retreats where acorns and pinecones are abundant. Regardless, most can come to enjoy the displacement for a few years, provided they live close to a park, a neighborhood garden, or a lesbian couple.

 The Three Types of Wiggers

TRIGGERS (Idio Rank: 5.1)

Triggers are the most predominant type of wigger (commonly associated with the rapper Eminem and Vanilla Ice). Triggers try to dress "street" by wearing oversized jerseys, do-rags, and showy jewelry. They pick up slang from MTV's *Cribs* and feign insider knowledge about the Bloods, the Crips, and the Biggie/Tupac conspiracy. When people talk about wiggers, they're usually referring to the Trigger genus.

BLINGERS (Idio Rank: 5.1)

Blingers are Triggers who have matured and now prefer designer suits, as worn by aging rappers like Jay-Z and P. Diddy. They feel they have entered a more serious phase in life and know that wearing Sean Jean suits with French cuffs, driving Lexuses, and accessorizing with oversized gold chains helps them foster a more serious and mature persona. Plus, the bitches give it up for the bling, yo.

G-WASPS (Idio Rank: 6.8)

G-WASPs are white intellectuals who are obsessed with black culture. They decorate their homes with African masks and statues, collect Rastafarian tapestries, and listen to Paul Simon, Bob Marley, and Ladysmith Black Mambazo. Many wear clothing with Jamaican- or African-themed prints. G-WASPs never use street slang but argue tooth and nail that Ebonics should be recognized as a valid form of linguistic study. Many become obsessed with tried-and-true black icons like Muhammad Ali, Malcolm X, Maya Angelou, and Martin Luther King Jr. Most don't like hip-hop but respect the heck out of it as a valid form of street poetry reflecting the turmoil of today's African American youth. Especially the work of Will Smith and Arrested Development. Though G-WASPs rarely dress like rappers, many males wear a diamond earring in their left ear to show that they're down with the G. Some braid their hair in cornrows.

UNCLE TOMATOES (Idio Rank: 4.9)

Anyone who has seen *The Godfather* or watched an episode of *The Sopranos* is familiar with the Mafioso stereotypes associated with Italian Americans. Though many Italians take offense at the gangster clichés associated with their culture, others embrace the mob image by dressing in tracksuits, wearing pinkie rings, and feigning New York or New Jersey accents. Italian women often conform to the stereotypes by sporting big, teased-out hair and painting their fingernails with gaudy designs. Some Italians decorate their homes and businesses by lovingly hanging pictures of Michael Corleone, Al Pacino, and Joey from *Friends* next to the Madonna.

Uncle Tomatoes, on the other hand, resent the wiseguy stereotypes and do everything in their power to defy them. They think crime families like the Gambinos, Genoveses, Luccheses, Bonannos, and the Colombos are made up of thugs and should not be romanticized as men of honor. Hearing the phrase "I'm gonna make you an offer you can't refuse" causes Uncle Tomatoes to seethe with rage.

Not surprisingly, many Uncle Tomatoes are teased within their own communities for acting too WASPy. After all, driving the family to Sal's pizzeria in a Volvo station wagon instead of a black Cadillac can be a point of dissension. Many send their children to their rooms should they begin gesturing too enthusiastically with their hands or make the mistake of saying "bada bing bada boom" at the dinner table. Other Uncle Tomatoes lecture their aunts, moms, and sisters on the inappropriateness of face pinching. More extreme cases swear off cannolis and meatballs.

Most notably, Uncles Tomatoes all share a hatred of Frank Sinatra. Just hearing "I've Got You Under My Skin" does more than get under their skin. It gives them a rash. Since most Uncle Tomatoes have been subjected to his music for years by Mafia-stereotype-embracing friends and family, Sinatra has come to personify everything that is wrong with the world. Uncle Tomatoes who own their own restaurants and cafés prefer playing Patsy Cline or Ronnie Milsap to Tony Bennett and Frank Sinatra. They hang up pictures of positive role models like Ray Romano, Connie Chung, and Roy Rogers. Luckily, Uncle Tomatoes always have a built-in defense against criticism. They simply say, "You keep conforming to stereotypes . . . *I'll do it myyyyy Way*!"

An Uncle Tomato

26 | Yanknecks

IN BRIEF: Rebel-flag-waving rednecks who live outside the South

GENDER: Male or female

POPULATION SIZE: Moderately common

HABITAT: Tractor pulls, Kansas/Styx/ELO reunion tours

HOBBIES: Shootin' skeet down by the ole lighthouse

FAVORITE BOOKS: *God, Pepsi, and Groovin' on the High Side: Tales from the NASCAR Circuit*; *Nuke 'Em*

IDIO RANK: 7.7

Overview

Ever been passed on the interstate by a bright yellow Camaro with chrome hubcaps, a Confederate flag bumper sticker, and New Hampshire tags? If so, you've spotted a Yankneck. The growing population of Yanknecks in America goes to show that the simple joys of Skoal Bandits, NASCAR races, cheddar cheese meatloaf, and muddin' down by the power lines can't be contained to the states south of the Mason-Dixon Line. After all, why should the South have a monopoly on stonewashed jeans and rattails dyed with peroxide?

As any Yankneck will attest, the South has *already* risen again. In fact, it's risen all the way up to Maine, New Hampshire, and even New Yawk City. Nowadays, you don't have to travel to 'Bama to find people who have driveways filled with chickens. The culture and traditions of the Southern, Confederate-flag-waving redneck have taken Yankeeland by storm. Almost every bar on the Eastern seaboard now has a guy in a sleeveless plaid shirt standing by a pool table waiting to kick your ass.

What About Confederate-Flag-Waving Rednecks in the Midwest, West Coast, and Elsewhere?

Though the name "Yankneck" is derived from combining the terms "Yankee" and "redneck," Yanknecks can be found in the Midwest and on the West Coast as well. This seeming contradiction comes from the fact that true Southern Confederates consider anyone who doesn't live beneath the Mason-Dixon Line to be a Yankee. The exception of course being Californians, who they classify as "fruits." It should be noted that Southerners who drink lattes or eat sushi are also called Yankees by more traditional Southern rednecks.

The Secret Lives of Yanknecks

Until now, the culture and origin of the Yankneck have been cloaked in mystery. Scientists who have tried to study them have often been chased off their property by Uncle Earl or the Evans boys. Following years of devoted research, we have finally succeeded in a thorough documentation of their noble ways.

Why do Yanknecks always decorate with Confederate flags?

Since the Stars and Bars are considered to be a controversial part of *Southern* heritage, many can't help but wonder why someone in Minnesota would want to wear a rebel flag bandanna or fly the Southern Cross on their property. Do they want to secede from the Union? To the new generation of rebel-flag wavers, the meaning of the Civil War–era banner has become much more nuanced. People who identify with the rebel flag today are attempting to communicate a complex set of ideas and opinions that have little to do with geography or history.

The Core Beliefs of Today's Rebel-Flag Waver, Part 1:

▶ If you look at my girlfriend, my sister, me, or my hunting dog, I have the God-given right to kick your ass.
▶ Though *Real Men Don't Eat Quiche* was written twenty years ago, it still resonates today.

- A real man provides a home for his family with a view of the interstate.
- Pink Floyd laser shows are best experienced drunk or high.
- Jim Beam and George Dickel are among our greatest Americans.
- The film industry's pinnacle achievement was *Cannonball Run II*.
- Family vacations should always involve a visit to Six Flags or a gun show.
- The term "liberal" is a synonym for a God-hating, Jewish, sushi-eating, homosexual New Yorker.

Why do Yanknecks speak with Southern accents?

Like anyone else, Yanknecks are influenced by pop culture, often emulating the customs and habits of their heroes and the people they see on TV. Since Yanknecks grow up watching fishing shows, Burt Reynolds movies, NASCAR races, and listening to Bocephus on the radio, it only makes sense that they would pick up the dialect and vernacular. There *are* subtle differences, though, in the dialects and idioms used by rednecks and Yanknecks. Yanknecks inevitably develop hybrid accents, blending their local dialects with a Southern drawl. Notice the subtle differences:

> **Boston Yankneck**—I'm fixin' ta go down to the rivah to get us some dinnah.
>
> **Southern Redneck**—I reckon' some scrod or crawdiddies would be right nice. I'm gonna set right heeya and watch the races while'n you go.
>
> **New York Yankneck**—Fuggetahboutit. I'll order some Eye-talian food or somethin' from the Great Americun House uh Poik.

What are the key differences and similarities between Yanknecks and rednecks?

Rednecks in the South are known for taking their own sweet time when it comes to doing almost anything. It can take them hours to jack up a pickup truck or iron a sheet for a Klan rally. Yanknecks, on the other hand, are accustomed to a faster pace of life. They consider time to be a valuable commodity and can change a diaper on a table at Mickey D's before you can finish your Big Mac.

Nevertheless, when it comes to most things in life, the similarities between rednecks and Yanknecks are striking. Both enjoy impressing the ladies with their cars. Nothing's sexier than popping the hood to reveal a 325 horsepower centrifugal supercharge system that propels fifteen pounds of boost through its box-mounted 950 cfm fuel meter. They both enjoy going to chili cook-offs and adding complexity to their recipes with a touch of rabbit or possum. They both wonder why the most recent Iraq war didn't have a cool T-shirt line, like Desert Storm. And though many Yanknecks like the Giants and the Bulls, most can't shake the feeling that they should be pulling for the Cowboys or the Hawks.

Are Yanknecks racists?

Of course not. They have stopped using the offensive N word in favor of "negra." As many Yanknecks will attest, they like negras and even used to work with a couple of 'em down at Roy's Discount Muffler Land.

Why do people choose to become Yanknecks in the first place?

Yanknecks generally have displaced Southern parents who teach them the ways of the redneck as children. They grow up eating supper on telephone cable spools and learn that any respectable home has the shell of a Mustang convertible displayed on cinder blocks.

Adolescent males simultaneously develop an appreciation for cars and women while staring at models posing with chrome carburetors in *Harley Bitches*. They learn from their dads that WD-40 provides superior hold for all hair types. They're taught the elegance of Izod shirts with Winston, Goodwrench, and Castrol GTX logos.

Adolescent females are instructed that the perfect pair of jeans is one size too tight to button. Showing the fellas that they're only a zipper away from some good country lovin' is the best way to distinguish yourself from the pack. They also discover that generously applying Aquanet can make even the flattest hair look stiff and fancy, like a top-dollar wig bought in the city.

Other Yanknecks become intrigued with the culture of rednecks on their own and begin buying Travis Tritt records and dipping Copenhagen. Yanknecks who have God-given names like Maybelle, Junior, Mary Jo, or Cale often feel they simply have no other choice but to fulfill their redneck destinies.

The Yankneck conspiracy

Many believe that there are subliminal messages and backward-masking on records by Peter Frampton, Garth Brooks, Guns N' Roses, The Scorpions, and Hank Williams Jr. These hidden messages have allegedly led multitudes of troubled youth down the path to becoming Yanknecks. Though the evidence is circumstantial, a remarkable 81 percent of all Yanknecks own a copy of Poison's "Every Rose Has Its Thorn," which, when digitally slowed down, contains the following hidden message:

> *Monster truck shows are awesome, oh beloved dark one. I will wear stonewashed jeans and grow a mullet. Sweet Satan, Sweet Satan. I will treat my lover to Red Lobster. Beer-battered buffalo wings and frozen Piña Coladas as big as your torso go well with lobster. My snake-toothed demon lord.*

SERFERS (Idio Rank: 5.6)

Serfers are wealthy intellectuals who have class guilt (similar to the Paleface Guilt of the Cherohonkee—see page 157) They're frustrated by people who network, talk about stock options, drink wine instead of beer, and compare résumés over dinner. In protest, they surf (as suggests the double meaning of their name) from one class to the next by striking up conversations with waiters, shaking hands with the postman, and saying hello to the "less shallow" blue-collar workers like Roy the garbageman. Treating them like people, they know, can tear down the barriers of elitism and classism. To show that they're in touch with the common man, Serfers insist upon flying coach and make a point of playing Bruce Springsteen when the plumber stops by to fix the drain.

Serfers are often depressed by how meaningless their white-collar jobs are and begin wearing baseball caps or cowboy hats to show their admiration of the proletariat. They never mention their work or the college they attended when they run into less successful people since everyone is equal in the Brotherhood of Man. Many Serfers become defensive if they hear people making jokes about trailer parks or questioning the value of unions. Some Serfers even adopt a blue-collar worker, like the guy who landscapes their lawn, as a friend. The conversational parallels that can be drawn between easy maintenance centipede grass and Roth IRAs are riveting.

Is NASCAR important to Yankneck culture?

Of course. Surprising to most is the fact that New Hampshire and even California have their own high-profile tracks. Unfortunately, Maine and Oregon are yet to build their own speedways, given their strict environmental bans on non-biodegradable beer cosies. Since the joy of NASCAR racing truly comes in the tailgate parties, Yanknecks who don't live close to racetracks are often forced to form their own tailgate parties back in the old field behind the high school.

Are Click and Clack, the hosts of *Car Talk*, Yanknecks?

No. They're considered to be communists by most Yanknecks since they work for the liberals, Jews, and pansies at NPR. Like al-Quaeda, Click and Clack hate freedom.

The Core Beliefs of Today's Rebel-Flag Waver, Part 2:

▶ Not having a vanity plate, mud flaps, and a big-screen TV is un-American.

▶ Jokes about poodle Szechuan are funny when dining at a Chinese restaurant.

▶ Sheriff Jenkins sure is book smart.

▶ Stone Cold Steve Austin, Ronald Reagan, Bocephus, Richard Petty, and Dale Earnhardt should be on Mount Rushmore.

▶ Iron Butterfly and Foghat are DEEPLY underrated.

▶ The words "Gentlemen, start your engines" are among the loveliest in the English language.

▶ In my book, "love it or leave it" really says it all.

▶ It just ain't a proper wedding without Cheez Whiz and pigs in a blanket.

27 | Cherohonkees

IN BRIEF: White baby boomers who are obsessed with Native American culture

GENDER: Male or female

POPULATION SIZE: Moderately rare

HABITAT: West Coast, Southwest, preferably in adobe homes

HOBBIES: Hosting drum circles, making chamomile tea, dancing with wolves

FAVORITE BOOKS: *Boston Brahman by Birth, Apache by the Grace of God*; *The Dummies Guide to Turquoise and Basket Weaving*

IDIO RANK: 7.8

Overview

Cherohonkees are a special breed of New Age baby boomers who have a unique affinity for turquoise jewelry, wolves, and Native American culture. They're found mainly in California and the Southwest but can adapt to any environment provided there's a macrobiotic restaurant close by and space for an herb garden. Most prefer living in the country or in close proximity to a liberal-minded town that hasn't been spoiled by McDonald's, the Gap, Wal-Mart, and the other scourges of the white man.

Cherohonkees believe that Americans have lost their understanding of the interconnectedness of all things. They begin emulating the traditional cultures of Native Americans in protest of the postindustrial pillaging of the earth. Though most Cherohonkees encourage clean living, some used to tour with The Dead or work at head shops with names like Scarlet Begonias and Mexicali Blues.

Paleface Guilt

Cherohonkees have a unique type of white guilt (usually associated with black slavery). They share the Native American's respect for Mother Earth and feel frustrated by the moral and spiritual shortcomings of their own people. Unable to identify with WASP culture and heritage, Cherohonkees have an inherent aversion to argyle sweaters, chipped beef, and khakis.

Despite the good intentions of the Cherohonkee, Native Americans rarely embrace the community. Insensitive Native American teens who don't understand the Cherohonkee's fascination with their culture have been known to refer to them as wiggers and crack jokes about thunder sticks and saltine pow-wows at this well-meaning group's expense.

Keeping It Real

All Cherohonkees love nature and often develop leathery skin from spending too much time outdoors. A weathered appearance makes them feel like they're keeping it real. Plus, immersing oneself in nature makes it easier to seek the counsel of the Wind. Cherohonkees take pride in their ability to spot poison oak or the tracks of a deer, an animal whose relationship to the Shape-Shifting Stag Man has been well documented in Cherohonkee lore.

Cherohonkees rarely own televisions and usually dispense with their Earth Day T-shirts and moccasins when at home since they prefer relaxing in the nude. Setting aside some quality naked time every day is a great way to rebel against one's Protestant heritage. All enjoy crafts such as making feather jewelry or painting fish to use as T-shirt prints. The truly happy Cherohonkee lives close to a fast-running stream where he can clean his crystals and turquoise jewelry.

Note: Cleaning with Brita water works too, but just feels less transcendental.

Jock Teases and First-Basers

JOCK TEASES (Idio Rank: 5.9)

Jock Teases couldn't care less about sports but follow the games from afar to win the affection of men. They know that the key to a sports fan's heart rarely lies in his stomach. The key to his heart sits on top of a table in his den and is tuned to ESPN. Single Jock Teases show up at sports bars and yell at the screen along with the other dudes. *"Get the ball. Come on, goddamnit. You're playing like a girl!"* Many drink beer and eat meat-lover's pizza to further the illusion. They know that the guys will all be thinking, *Wow, that chick's really cool*, and use this to gain advantage in the competitive singles world. Married Jock Teases know that

wearing an oversized jersey on Sunday when their husband's friends all arrive to watch the Raiders is a surefire way to get everyone's attention. Sometimes Jock Teases make the first move by grabbing a man's hand during a high five and then holding on to it for the rest of the game.

FIRST-BASERS (Idio Rank: 4.1)

Like Jock Teases, First-Basers have little if any interest in sports. They simply feel pressured to read the sports section in order to avoid being ostracized at work. Knowing that the most popular water cooler topic is often sports, many First-Basers worry they'll be passed over for the next promotion should they not stay up-to-date with all the stats. First-Basers catch the tail end of the important games and take notes during the sports recap on the eleven o'clock news so they can engage in conversation confidently. Nevertheless, it's hard to compete with the office sports nut, who charms everyone with fun sports recaps and interpretative reenactments of end zone dances. Many First-Basers get busted when the wives of the people they're trying to deceive run into them at Bed Bath & Beyond after they've claimed they'll be watching a play-off game.

The Grounded Cherohonkee

Cherohonkees find peace in nature-based religions, and when writing, place words like "The Way," "Mountain Stream," and "Yellow Jacket" in capital letters to show their reverence. Despite their admiration for Native American culture, Cherohonkees are an open-minded people and know that truth can be found in all religions. They tend to seek out wisdom wherever they can find it and embrace any religion that mentions "grounding and centering," "gestating," or the "ebb and flow." The spiritual powers of love, dreamcatchers, and "John Tesh Live at Red Rocks" are transcendent.

The Life Journey

Cherohonkees consider life to be the Great Adventure and refer to their experiences as their "life journeys." Most enjoy writing and keep life journey notebooks in lieu of diaries. Though reading another's diary is always an invasion of privacy, reading a Cherohonkee's life journal can, according to mythology, unleash the fury of the Grass People.

Cherohonkees incorporate spirituality and profundity into all aspects of their lives. Many Cherohonkees designate "ethereal realms" for meditation in their homes by cleansing them (known as smudging) with burning sage. Others place *I'd Rather Be Spirit Drumming* bumper stickers on their Volvos. Many Cherohonkees assemble medicine wheels (meditative spots created by assembling stones into a circle and sprinkling the area with maize) in their backyards. In the absence of maize, corn-based Rain Forest Crunch is an acceptable substitution.

The Cherohonkee Zealot

More religious Cherohonkees often attempt to contact totemic animals, powerful beings that visit during meditation time in the form of wild beasts to instruct and provide wisdom. Salmon are associated with perseverance and renewal. Wolves are loyal mentors. Honeybees are nourishers of the soul. The Bear is the guardian of the Earth's heart chakra. Few Cherohonkees feel any kinship with Blue Jays. Everyone knows that Blue Jays are assholes. Not surprisingly, the most common totem for the Cherohonkee is the WASP.

When visited by a totemic animal, Cherohonkees usually bestow them with gifts. If visited by the Wolf, Cherohonkees offer up a poem, sage, or some fragrant incense. Bad gifts for the Wolf include kibble, Crazy Horse Malt Liquor, and gum.

To learn more about totems we recommend reading *Dog-Headed Buffalo Harmonics for Caucasians*. More vigorous spiritual explorers may prefer *Extreme Dog-Headed Buffalo Harmonics for Caucasians*.

Cherohonkees often discover that having a talking stick is conducive to a healthy marriage. According to ancient Native American tradition, whoever is holding the talking stick has free reign to speak without interruption. Some have been known to use them inappropriately to prevent their spouses from getting a word in edgewise: "Stanley, I mean Tall Bear, don't interrupt me. *I'm* holding the talking stick."

Cherohonkees also incorporate spiritual lingo into their daily lives. When giving advice they begin by saying "we human beings" and prefer holding hands while talking to add a level of earnestness. Others turn the runes and the tarot into verbs, asking friends "Did you runes that?" should an important decision need to be made.

In a Tribe of Their Own

The Cherohonkees' kindness, open-mindedness, and impressive herb gardens make them a great people to know should you ever need a steadfast friend or a good juniper connection. Regardless, the life of the Cherohonkee is often filled with strife. Cherohonkees who have close-minded parents are often subject to insensitive remarks like "We're dining at the club with your cousins tonight. Do you mind not dressing like a freakin' injun?"

28 | Hexpatriates

IN BRIEF: Expatriates who never actually ever leave the country. They just speak ill of (hex) America's corruption and lack of refinement.

GENDER: Male or female

POPULATION SIZE: Moderately common

HABITAT: Truffaut film festivals, gallery openings, BBC America, the United Colors of Benetton

HOBBIES: Collecting film noir and forties propaganda posters, practicing the French inhale

IDIO RANK: 6.2

The German Cup

The French Sophisti-hale

British Soccer Hooligan

The French Inhale

Hexpatriates try to look European when they smoke.

Overview

Hexpatriates believe that American culture has been going down the bidet for a long time now. Americans are too fat, too lazy, too arrogant, and most of all just too bloody American. People in the United States want everything to be easy and think that there needs to be a Gap and a McDonald's on every corner. Even though Hexpatriates were born in the US of A, they want nothing to do with this vulgar and politically arrogant country. In any given conversation they're sure to reference one of the following:

▶ America's need for socialized health care and stronger language programs
▶ How Europeans get to take naps
▶ The importance of public transportation and the corruption of the oil industry
▶ The harms of antibacterial soap
▶ America's lack of appreciation for the arts and architecture
▶ How yummy mayo tastes with fries

Hexpatriates all hate American TV and watch *The Office*, *What Not to Wear*, *Benny Hill*, and *Monty Python* to fine-tune their understanding of life overseas. When talking politics they make a point of saying "If we have another four years like the last, I am *definitely* moving abroad."

(**Note:** Hexpatriates are usually obsessed with European culture, but see EastPatriates on page 166 for Asian-obsessed Hexpatriates.)

Signs You Are a Hexpatriate, Part 1:

▶ You think "European" is a synonym for "elegant," similar to the way "American" is a synonym for "dumbass."
▶ You hold firmly to the belief that ketchup is bourgeois.
▶ You become very enthusiastic when introducing your international friends to others and still have your eyes open for an Australian.
▶ You practice your pronunciation of "croissant" before going to brunch.
▶ You're a huge fan of at least one of the following: Serge Gainsbourg, Noam Chomsky, Bridgette Bardot, Jeanne Moreau, Truffaut, or Catherine Deneuve.
▶ You sign your letters with "cheers," "best," or "ciao."
▶ When overseas, you pretend to be Canadian.

Beacons of Light

Hexpatriates love Rome for its history, Venice for its romance, Madrid for its vitality, and London for its refinement. Most of all, Hexpatriates love Paris for its overall cultural superiority. Many Hexpatriates are experts on France because of that trip they took freshman year. Recently, many Hexpatriates have begun to consider adopting Spain as their new favorite country. After all, that *New York Times* story about how *in vogue* Spanish cuisine has become was pretty convincing. Nevertheless, many still get a chill when they hear the French national anthem.

Hexpatriates consider themselves to be worldly jet-setters, beacons of light to our geography-ignorant republic. They're the enlightened few who actually care about world politics, as reported by the BBC. They get giddy discussing the growth of the euro and are happy to pay a little extra now when traveling overseas.

It is a given that Hexpatriates have world maps on their walls. Knowing exactly where Haiti is on the globe enables them to comprehend all the cultural richness and nuances of the country's culture. Some even read up on other countries, should they become tired of discussing Middle East oil conspiracies, the fattening of America, French cinema, or Nutella.

Many Hexpatriates blame air conditioners for single-handedly destroying outdoor café culture and consider large suburban lawns (that are never actually used for anything) more evil than Styrofoam. Older Hexpatriates insist on taking their children to the opera, though their kids would rather see *The Lion King on Ice*.

L'Art de Vivre

Hexpatriates personify *l'art de vivre* (the art of living well) and always know which wines, cuisine fusions, and leather footwear are fashionable in any given season. They uniformly avoid movies with explosions and car chases in favor of celluloid classics that feature more sophisticated ingredients like midgets and circuses. French auto-racing films are A-OK in their book though.

Hexpatriates love coffee but are very particular about how it's served. It enrages them when their cappuccino is delivered with a spoon inside the mug and only Sugar in the Raw is acceptable. Should you decide to make a pit stop at Starbucks, the Hexpatriate will voice a subtle protest by waiting outside.

Most importantly, Hexpatriates would never choose Wal-Mart over Target, or *Tar-jay,* as it's become known. After all, Wal-Mart doesn't look out for its employees. A philosophical understanding of the plight of the proletariat, they know, is integral to being intellectually progressive. More proactive Hexpatriates sometimes wear soccer shirts to the mall to illustrate that they're down with unions, blue-collar workers, and the common man.

Others are fashion elitists and have a natural aversion to shorts, jackets that are not made of leather, and sneakers. Deep down, many Hexpatriates are self-loathing and not comfortable inside their own skins. They think to themselves, *Maybe if I'd had an endearing European accent, my dad would have loved me more.*

MACTRESSES (Idio Rank: 5.3)

Mactresses are models who think they're actresses because they played the lead in *Grease* in high school. Despite the money they make doing shoots for the JCPenny catalog and the rave reviews of the off-Broadway show they did five years ago, they aspire to become even *more* established in their careers by securing a spot on a soap opera or in a Fruit Roll-Ups commercial. More accomplished Mactresses secure agents who know all the important boob-job doctors and can provide them with advice on how to get skinnier. Even though their idea of a demanding role is holding a smile for an hour while posing with a bottle of nail polish remover, they all claim (with great pride) to be actors. In reality, most spend their days working in coffee shops or waiting to hear back about that great gig hosting a South Beach dating show.

Signs You Are a Hexpatriate, Part 2:

▶ You insist upon calling the bathroom the water closet or the loo, even when you're at The Great American Steakhouse.

▶ When complaining about how ugly U.S. currency is, you try to do so with a British accent.

▶ You insist upon having your salad after the main course.

▶ You inform the cashier at A&P that Europeans bring their own bags before making a decision between paper and plastic.

▶ You can think of no harsher word in the English language than "Republican."

▶ You instantly take a liking to people who greet you with a kiss to both cheeks.

▶ You wonder why people often miss your amusing references to *Fawlty Towers*.

▶ You're considering adopting an Asian baby.

Hexperanto (Esperanto for Hexpatriates)

Since most Hexpatriates have great respect for the French, it's not surprising that they sprinkle their conversations with words and phrases borrowed from the language of love. When greeting a friend they commonly say "bonjour" (or "allo" when answering the phone) and integrate a couple of phrases like "joie de vivre" into their vocabulary. Nevertheless, Hexpatriates are rarely fluent in any language other than English. As they will tell you: "What do you expect, I'm a stupid American."

But they do uniformly attempt to use more international-sounding words, even when they sound awkward. When meeting someone new, they inquire, "So where did you go to university?" knowing that the word "college" is just too American. Some refer to the Loews multiplex at the mall as "the cinema" and the Motel Six by Hardees as "the pensión."

Most commonly, Hexpatriates try to internationalize the way they communicate by incorporating British slang into their vocabularies. They know saying things like "If I see another bloody flag, I'm gonna shite myself" just makes them appear more worldly. Some intentionally use more obscure slang to impress those around them, saying things like "Their bangers and mash are stonking, innit!" Most felt a little undermined when Austin Powers introduced the word "shag" to everyone else.

Like the French, who are notoriously impatient with mispronunciations of their language, Hexpatriates won't talk to other *English* speakers if they enunciate with an overly Southern twang. Hexpatriates work hard at getting rid of their own accents and have no patience with anyone who pronounces "nuclear" *nucular.*

To their credit, most Hexpatriates *are* **menu-multilinguals** and can order a glass of Chianti in several languages. When they do go overseas, they spend most of their time with other Americans. Most locals tire quickly of their transparent attempts to win favor by saying America sucks.

Signs You Are a Hexpatriate, Part 3:

If you regularly use two or more of the following terms, you could be a Hexpatriate:

flat (apartment)	biscuit (cookie)
bloke (man)	chips, crisps (fries and potato chips)
arse, bum (instead of ass)	wanker (idiot)
A to Z (map)	take the piss (make fun of)
bloody (similar to "damn")	slag (slut)
knickers in a twist (get upset)	bugger (sodomize)
preggers (pregnant)	nappy (diaper)
fag (cigarette)	crumpet (sexy woman)
jumper (sweater)	telly (television)
knickers (underwear)	blimey
arse over tit (head over heels)	rubbish (trash, nonsense)
row (fight)	oy (like "yo")

EastPatriates

Though not as common, some Hexpatriates are obsessed with Asian culture. They find meaning in the comparatively inverse way Asians perceive the world and often enjoy wearing kimonos and growing ponytails. EastPatriates are riveted by Eastern religions and decorate their homes with Buddha statues, yin-yang iconography, and think eating a raw foods diet is the way of the Tao. More nerdy EastPatriates are fans of anime, kung fu movies, and decorate their mantles with mounted samurai swords. All EastPatriates enjoy incorporating the word "zen" into casual conversation.

Yakovs, Eurotards, Desserters, and Casserole Pan Asians

Yakovs, Eurotards, Desserters, and Casserole Pan Asians are people from the USSR, Europe, the Middle East, and Asia, respectively, who readily embrace staple Americana like Disneyland, Wonder Bread, Elvis, SUVs, and Kentucky Fried Chicken. Similar to Hexpatriates, they have little appreciation for their own homelands. They speak ill of their own country's traditions in favor of American culture and Jell-O with stuff in it.

ENIGMATARDS (Idio Rank: 5.6)

Enigmatards are vegan animal-rights activists who wear lots of leather. Leather sneakers, jackets, backpacks, and sometimes even pants are commonly worn by Enigmatards. They refuse to acknowledge the contradictions, despite their devotion to *Fast Food Nation* and their tendency to go on tirades about how eating bovine flesh is barbaric. When asked to explain the difference between eating and wearing animal products, they change the subject by asking "Did you know Twinkies have beef products in their filling?" Others play the pleather card, suggesting that they're wearing imitation leather. Some defend themselves saying they wear only free-range leather.

29 | Winkies

IN BRIEF: Gay Evangelical Christians
GENDER: Either
POPULATION SIZE: Moderately rare
HABITAT: The Bible closet
FAVORITE BOOKS: The Left Behind Series, The Lubricated Behind Series
FAVORITE BIBLE TRANSLATIONS: New International Version (NIV), The Sodom and Gomorrah Bible (S&G)
IDIO RANK: 6.8

Overview: The Fundamentalist

One in eight people are gay, so it only makes sense that one in eight Fundamentalist Christians would be gay as well. Most Christian churches these days offer an unofficial "don't ask, don't tell" policy with regard to gays and lesbians, but the Fundamentalist church is a very different creature altogether. Primarily found in the South and in places where rattlesnakes are indigenous, Fundamentalists believe the Bible should be accepted at face value and interpreted literally. They take pride in the fact that they don't pick and choose when it comes to understanding God's teachings. They follow the *whole* Bible. Even the creepy parts.

The Fundamentalist church's devotion has earned them the blessed privilege of direct communication with Jesus. Thanks to the correspondences that evangelicals such as Jimmy Swaggart, David Wilkerson, Pat Robertson, and John Ashcroft have had with the Lord, we know today that the Lord despises homosexuality, votes Republican, speaks with a Southern accent, uses hairspray, and has stock in several multinational oil companies in Jesus' homeland.

Overview: The Winkie

Despite the Fundamentalist church's staunch opposition to homosexuality, it's not surprising that many Winkies are drawn to evangelical Christianity even though they're forced to be secretive about their sexuality. After all, they don't call it *FUN*-damentalism for nothing! Most gays who live in communities where Fundamentalism thrives stay in the closet anyway to avoid being dragged behind pickup trucks. Holding a little "you're-going-to-hell" talk against the Fundamentalist church just seems a tad silly.

Despite rumors to the contrary propagated by agents of the Beast, Fundamentalists are social progressives. They observe a strict "love thy neighbor" stance with regard to all people. Even Catholics! They would never harm a gay or lesbian, as long as they don't get too close to their children. And though no *true* Christian would endorse gay marriage, most Fundamentalists believe that gays have every right to be hired (with equal pay) as cooks at Burger King, provided they wear gloves to prevent the spread of HIV and sexually transmitted disease.

Virginity Is A-OK

Most gays and lesbians are initially drawn to the Christian church for the same reasons that heterosexuals find it appealing: it's a great place to meet naïve virgins.

Male Winkies often attend church for leisure purposes. Where else can you go to sing in a choir, play the handbells, perform synchronized dance routines in Christmas pageants, and be surrounded by guys with mustaches? Others simply want to fulfill a fantasy of saying "Will you lay hands on me, Deacon Jones?" Conforming to all the rules can be difficult, especially since wearing Prada and

Questions That Perplex Male Winkies

- ▶ Do these shoes go with my Bible?
- ▶ Does this church have a gym?
- ▶ What's a good Rapture outfit?
- ▶ Does Tower Records have a Contemporary Christian house music section?
- ▶ Why does Communion have to have so many carbs?
- ▶ Is it a sin to use anointing oil with my partner?
- ▶ Wouldn't Fire and Brimstone be a hot name for a club?
- ▶ The ladies have bingo, why can't we have baths?
- ▶ Why didn't Jesus get a better fashion consultant?

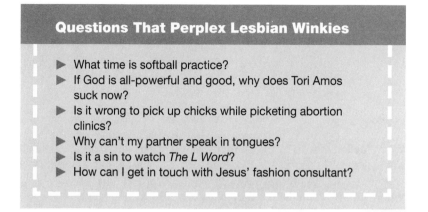

Questions That Perplex Lesbian Winkies

▶ What time is softball practice?
▶ If God is all-powerful and good, why does Tori Amos suck now?
▶ Is it wrong to pick up chicks while picketing abortion clinics?
▶ Why can't my partner speak in tongues?
▶ Is it a sin to watch *The L Word*?
▶ How can I get in touch with Jesus' fashion consultant?

shopping at Barneys defies the Christian dress code. Jesus prefers T.J. Maxx and stores that specialize in polyblend suits. Commonly, their secrets are discovered when they bring foie gras or butternut squash soup to the church picnic instead of fried chicken or broccoli and Kraft cheese casserole. Male Winkies think Jezebel, Bathsheba, the Madonna, and Amy Grant are total divas.

Lesbian Winkies are often attracted to Fundamentalist churches because the tambourines and acoustic guitars remind them of the Lilith tour. Others become titillated by the stiff, highlighted hairdos they see on the *700 Club* and want to go somewhere that they can meet hot Fundamentalist bitches. Fundamentalists also have a much laxer dress code than the Baptists, and lesbian Winkies feel right at home wearing baseball caps and sandals to Sunday school.

Both gay and lesbian Winkies become adept at changing the subject when the church busybody tries to set them up with nice Christian girls and boys, respectively.

Note: Winkies should remember to use the Christian fish insignia to cover any rainbow stickers on their cars. If someone still discovers that you're gay, claim you're demon possessed or merely backsliding.

Fitting In: Rules That Apply to Everyone

Regardless of sexual orientation, the rules are more or less the same for gays and straights who are attending a Fundamentalist church. Here are some key things to keep in mind to assure you'll fit in.

1. Hand raising

To show moderate praise: Raise your hands to breast level with your palms in the air. Doing so indicates that you're a believer and know the rules. People who fail to perform the minimal amount of hand raising in church may cause suspicion.

Moderate praise   Moved by the spirit   Jesus-induced convulsions

When feeling moved by the spirit: Raise your hands to the top of your head with outstretched palms. Mix things up a bit by gently throwing a fist, like a cheerleader doing a hooray cheer.

When feeling Jesus-induced convulsions: Extend your hands all the way up above your head with your palms toward heaven. Tilting your head back and looking upward can imply your anointed place in the Kingdom.

Note: In all cases, open eyes suggest excitement. Closed eyes suggest you've made contact with the Holy Spirit. Always refrain from doing jazz hands during worship.

2. Socializing
End each statement by randomly naming a Bible verse such as Ephesians 16:12 to show that your words have biblical backing. Ending your sentences with a pointed "in accordance with prophecy" or "so sayeth the Lord" can help add spiritual credibility.

3. Snake handling
We recommend bringing your own, nonpoisonous reptile. This emphasizes your devotion to the Lord, ensures your safety, and demonstrates that you're a go-getter.

4. When discussing homosexuality, what do I say?
"I don't hate homosexuals, I hate the sin." If in Texas, say, "I don't hate faggots and dykes, I just hate the sin."

5. Helpful props
Always carry a *worn* copy of the Bible (preferably one that zips shut) and a title from the Left Behind Series. Avoid carrying the King James Version (that's for English lit professors, poets, Presbyterians, and other sinners).

6. Show you're up on current events
Name-drop Christian power players like James Dobson, Pat Robertson, and that other dude who says "Jaaay-sus." Also make a point of discussing how *Harry Potter,* rap music, and *The Da Vinci Code* are tools of the Beast. To stand out from the crowd, say that you're boycotting *The Passion of the Christ* since Mel Gibson was in other godless movies like *Mad Max* and *Lethal Weapon.*

7. Talk the talk

Familiarize yourself with Christian buzzwords and idioms like "bless-ed," "filled with the spirit," "anointing," "full Gospel church," "prayer warrior," and "Halliburton." Be sure to find out if your church's preferred term for the dark one is Satan, the Beast, the devil, Lucifer, or Clinton.

8. Speaking in tongues

Practice speaking in tongues by saying quickly and repeatedly:
"I shoulda boughta Volvo, I coulda boughta Honda."

9. A special note for Winkies

Bring earplugs should the sermon be entitled "Christian Eye for the Unrepentant Deviant."

FAUXHEMIANS, POSTEREORS, AND INDIELECTUALS (Idio Rank: 6.3)

As defined by Idiosyncrological guidebook *The Hipster Handbook*, Hipsters are people who possess "tastes, social attitudes, and opinions deemed cool by the cool." However, Hipsters have largely begun to feel uncomfortable in their own skins, given the increased media attention to their demographic. Many Hipsters feel that their irony-laden aesthetic has been capitalized upon by Urban Outfitters and MTV. Not to mention the fact that many Hipsters have been exposed as **Fauxhemians,** wealthy "bohemians" who shop at Salvation Army to give the illusion that they're roughing it. All in all, most Hipsters feel a bit exposed and vulnerable these days. Given the growing amount of Hipster backlash, a new breed of Hipster known as the **Postereor** (short for Post Stereotype) has begun to emerge. Postereors all dress like Hipsters, listen to indie music, smoke Parliaments, join kitschy cover bands, and complain that Ugg boots are totally over. But when asked whether or not they're Hipsters, Postereors become belligerent and inform you that they most certainly are not. Postereors also say things like "Care Bear T-shirts are hot" but are sure to follow this up with a pointed "and I'm not being kitschy" to distinguish themselves from Hipsters.

IndieLectuals are never fond of being called Hipsters either. They believe that Hipsters are spoiled trendy brats, whereas they're individuals who are blessed with exquisite taste. Unlike fashion-obsessed Postereors, IndieLectuals throw out 90 percent of their overtly trendy attire (CHIPs sunglasses, seventies-style ski vests) to distance themselves from Hipster culture. Nevertheless, they maintain a touch of Hipster flair by holding on to their Chuck Taylors or by choosing a disheveled hairstyle. This ensures that they won't

be confused with your average square or working stiff should they step into a franchise restaurant by mistake. Like Hipsters, IndieLectuals possess ironic senses of humor and have a natural aversion to Tom Hanks. They are flush with knowledge on everything indie and can discern if something has become passé weeks before anyone else. Nevertheless, IndieLectuals insist they're neither hip nor trendy. "The scene" has gotten really lame these days, they attest. So who has the time to bother?

A Fauxhemian

30 | The Cryptster

IN BRIEF: Hipsters who are too old (one would think) to be concerned about being hip

GENDER: Male or female

POPULATION SIZE: Moderately common

HABITAT: Salvation Army, bars that have Ms. Pac-Man/Galaga or Big Buck Hunter 2

FAVORITE MUSIC: Genres of music with the prefixes "alt," "post," "grind," "math," "retro," "emo, and "post-alt-emo-math-grindcore"

IDIO RANK: Varies (see below)

Overview

In retrospect, just imagine how much better *Friends* would have been had they called it quits before the cast got wrinkled and old. They were one season away from a subplot about Phoebe's hot flashes and Chandler's swollen prostate when they finally ended things. Though few would mistake the cast of *Friends* for being hip, it's a perfect analogy for the plight of the Cryptster, aging Hipsters who fail to realize the time has come to throw in the ironic He-Man beach towel. Cryptsters don't understand that if you're over thirty and still wearing a Dickie's work shirt with someone else's name on it, people will assume you really *do* work the full-service pump at Amoco. And resting your baby seat on the pool table while you grab a pitcher just doesn't look very cool.

Though the aging process is difficult for everyone, Hipsters have an especially hard time adjusting. Their whole identity is based on being cutting edge and cool, terms that are usually synonymous with youth. Accepting the aging process defies their youthful instincts, but saying that they remember reading

Rolling Stone when it was relevant simply doesn't win them any status points with the younger, actually hip crew. Hipsters wondering if they've transformed into Cryptsters need only consider one fact: If you've ever pondered the question "Am I too old to be hip?" then you're more than likely a Cryptster.

The Core Types of Cryptsters

JETS (Idio Rank: 7)

Given their obsession with an antiquated New York street style, Jets are named for the *West Side Story* street gang. They fashion themselves after the Ramones and Patti Smith and, regardless of where they live, look longingly into the distance whenever anyone mentions CBGB. Because they can still fit into their favorite pair of skintight pants, Jets fail to realize they've aged. Wearing their pants tight from hip to ankle ensures that their speed doesn't fall out should they get a hole in the pocket. Jets become a tad wrinkled from chain-smoking and drinking, but they

Cryptster Checklist: Clues Your Ironic Exterior Has Passed Its Expiration Date

- ▶ You don't go to clubs anymore because you hate standing.
- ▶ You increase your blood pressure medicine on the weekend, in case you decide to do coke.
- ▶ Your beer gut is visible through your Ramones/Sonic Youth/Joy Division/Pavement T-shirt.
- ▶ You found some gray hairs in your fauxhawk.
- ▶ Your favorite outfit from high school was recently reissued by Urban Outfitters.
- ▶ You buy two pairs of Buddy Holly glasses, just in case they stop making them.
- ▶ You spent Saturday night washing lactation stains out of your wife's shirts.
- ▶ You recently caught yourself using the term "smart casual."
- ▶ You sometimes think to yourself, *Maybe cutting corporate taxes* would *stimulate the economy*.
- ▶ You claim to love emo but have no idea what the term means.
- ▶ You think Philip Glass, Gypsy Kings, Stereolab, and Laurie Anderson are cutting edge.

think it gives them a tough-as-leather mystique, like Lou Reed. It's hard to discern what Jets are saying sometimes since they slur their words, but if you respond to them with an enthusiastic "fuck yeah," they usually seem to be appeased. All Jets realize that wearing black punk rock T-shirts can be very intimidating and scary. In fact, elderly women from Iowa sometimes cross the street just to avoid them. After all, they could be carrying switchblades!

I-RONNIES (Idio Rank: 5.2)

I-Ronnies are male Cryptsters who get their name from their tendency to exclaim, "I'm over the whole irony thing." They've been immersed in the irony-laced Hipster scene for so long they claim they can't stand irony any longer. I-Ronnies were all glad to see the mesh baseball cap phenomenon lose steam since they were wearing them way back in the eighties. They know that the only timeless fashion trends are Buddy Holly glasses and messenger bags.

I-Ronnies age more gracefully than other Cryptsters since they *already* dress like they belong in a retirement home. They know that wearing polyester pants with a short-sleeve, button-down, thrift-shop shirt looks great no matter how old you are. Most ease up on the self-deprecating humor they were known for in their youths. They realize that facetiously saying "I'm such a loser" could potentially be misconstrued and taken at face value by others. Many claim to be the first person to ever stand in the front row of an indie show sullen and with his arms crossed.

THE ROUGE (Idio Rank: 5.2)

The Rouge is a female Cryptster who is very fond of kitschy, retro apparel and knee socks. She gets her name from her wine-stained teeth. She usually has a Betty Page haircut or a Linda Ronstadt mullet. Rouges focus on creating the perfect kitschy ambience for their homes. They're too old to go out regularly at night but still want to show the world that they're cutting edge. Their collections of Tikki glassware, sixties-style lamps, shag carpets, and ironic lunchboxes distracts others from noticing that they're looking a little heftier in their thrift-shop skirts these days. Buying a bike with a bell and basket can also help to take the attention off the aging process. And selecting the right kitschy band shirt, like Yes or Ratt, can do wonders when it comes to making them look younger.

Many Rouges enjoy showing off the 'zines they used to self-publish. The issues featuring the scribbly cat sold well back during the Grunge era, they inform younger Hipsters who aren't familiar with their work. When put on the spot by family members who worry they aren't realizing their potential, Rouges reassure them by relating their plans to open a restaurant or design their own clothing lines. Like I-Ronnies, Rouges claim to be over irony as well. They insist they *sincerely* like unicorns and rainbows when asked to explain the pattern on their jackets.

Sarah Jane Newbury

What's more unusual than a middle-aged virgin? How about a world-renowned middle-aged virgin with a doctor's note to prove that her hymen is still intact?

Sarah Jane Newbury is our second non-American CATSCAN (see Johanna Pieterman) and Britain's most famous virgin. She regularly appears in newspapers, magazines, and on talk shows to discuss her sexuality. Or lack thereof, rather. As she's fond of saying, she's "Virgo Intacta." Sarah Jane is a living testament that you can be over forty and a virgin by choice. As this self-proclaimed international celebrity claims, "I respect God's ideal plan that people should marry [and] have clean sex lives."

Throughout Sarah Jane's life, she's often had trouble convincing people that she's a virgin. She says that many have "spread rumors" and "slandered" her by claiming that she lies about her chastity. Coworkers, neighbors, and acquaintances have all too frequently declared that she lies to attract men with the prospect of deflowering her. Others have suggested that she must be a lesbian. A neighbor even asked her to not put her underwear on the clothesline, afraid that Sarah Jane was trying to seduce her husband.

These slanderous accusations convinced Sarah Jane she needed medical proof of her virginity. She decided to visit her gynecologist, who provided her with a note stating that she's "genuinely intact and that she has not had any plastic surgery." A local reporter caught wind of Sarah Jane's story, and her fame quickly followed.

Sarah now regularly visits her gynecologist to provide updated written proof to those who doubt her word. Sarah informs people on her Web site that anyone who wages "malicious attacks" against her assertions of being a virgin will be sued. She says she can provide tape recordings of people slandering her to prove she's not being paranoid about this allegedly recurring slander.

Sarah Jane has always wanted to get married but has simply not found the right man. She's had dozens of boyfriends (including "several millionaires" and one ten-year relationship). She's even had several offers of marriage. Neverthe-

less, she has stood firmly by her belief that people should wait until they're married to engage in sexual activity. And yes, this includes avoiding oral sex.

In addition to remaining chaste, which is undoubtedly a lot of work, Sarah Jane collects porcelain unicorns, cherubs, ducks, and lions for her garden. "Her nieces and nephews love to see them," not to mention the fact that they "help keep rats away." Sarah Jane is also "very impressed with the collection of frogs owned by a former Chairman of the District Council, which was displayed in his office." A very well-rounded lady indeed, Sarah Jane also enjoys shooting clay targets with a gun.

Along with Johanna, Sarah Jane goes to show that the study of Idiosyncrology can flourish beyond this idiosyncratic republic. Visit her today at www .sarahjanenewbury.com.

What Is Your Idio Type?

Are you so singular and distinctive that you're yet to be classified? Now's your chance to scientifically document yourself for posterity. Since it is impossible for someone to objectively define themselves, this test requires the aid of at least one friend, colleague, or family member who knows you well.

INSTRUCTIONS:
Part 1. Fill out the top five questions yourself, since they are objective in nature.
Part 2. Have your friend or friends complete this section.

Part 1: About You
▶ Your Name: _____
▶ Favorite Book: _____
▶ Favorite CD: _____
▶ Favorite Movie: _____
▶ Where you can usually be found: _____

Part 2: How People See You
▶ **Sex Appeal:** _____
    (Scale: 1 is the cat's litter box, 10 is the cat's meow)
▶ **Adjective that best describes** _____ : _____
                                              participant's name
▶ **If** _____ **was a doll with a pull string,** _____ **would**
        participant's name   participant's name

utter the following 3 phrases:
    1. _____
    2. _____
    3. _____

▶ **The most neurotic thing about** _____ **is the way**
                                            participant's name

he/she _____

Idio Type Name
(optional—accurate naming often requires professional Idiosyncrological training):

_____

31 | Idiosyncrologists

IN BRIEF: Scientists who neurotically classify, draw, and study human creatures

GENDER: Male or female

POPULATION SIZE: Rare

HABITAT: Brooklyn, The Pourhouse, JCPenney, Chuck E. Cheese, and other places where human droppings can be collected

IDIO RANK: 10

Robert Lanham: The Author

Robert Lanham is the author of the beach-towel classic known as *The Emerald Beach Trilogy* (*Pre-Coitus*, *Coitus*, and *Aftermath*). In 2003, he blindsided both the pop culture and anthropology worlds by simultaneously publishing the bestselling first two installments of the Idiosyncrological canon, *The Hipster Handbook* and *Cyborgs, Libertarians, and People Who Like Vin Diesel*. He is currently the editor of FREEwilliamsburg, which can be found online at www .freewilliamsburg.com. Robert lives in Brooklyn, New York, and is really muscular. In fact, it's kind of eerie how muscular he is. His ferret is Wiccan.

Jeff Bechtel: The Illustrator

Born in the backwaters and backwash of Indiana before relocating to New York, Jeff Bechtel is perpetually contemplating life's tough questions. Why can European magazines show nudity on their covers when American magazines cannot? Why do ceiling fans stop moving when strobe lights are flashing? And if lemons smell "lemony," why don't oranges smell "orangey." His work has appeared in *Guidepost*, *Better Homes and Gardens*, *Martha Stewart Living*, *Playboy*, *Beef Digest*, and "Marmaduke." Bechtel lives, works, and regularly plays canasta with elderly women in Brooklyn.

Trevor Hoey: The Art Adviser

Trevor Hoey secured a degree in Idiosyncrological Studies at Newark Community College. He was born in New York City, was raised in the Amish section of Villanova, Pennsylvania, and now lives in Manhattan, as per the request of the ladies. Prior to becoming an Idiosyncrologist, he was a traveling Olestra salesman. He claims to have a worldly pessimism but a personal cheeriness. He says a lot of weird shit like that though.

Mandy Novak: The Field Researcher

Mandy Novak does it all—documentary filmmaker, faith healer, director of *The Last Samurai*, and Idiosyncrologist extraordinaire. In her free time, Mandy enjoys quiet walks in the countryside, hang gliding, and offtrack betting. She lives in Brooklyn, New York, with a bulimic cat.

Creative Contributors: Matt Casper, Dan Kilian, Jud Laghi, Glenn Stevens
Special Thanks: Anna Brown, Joanna Burgess, Matt Byrnie, Colin Cheney, John Church, Judy Coan-Stevens, Sarah Cook, Anne Feve Jones, The Enviably Astute Kristen Fulton Wright, Haydar, Kevin Kraynick, Adrianne Lanham, Michelle Levy, Kimmy Loewe, Matt McLean, Chris Nespor, Bret Nicely, Cameron O'Brion, Rasha Refaie, John Rickman, Benjamin Stokes, Noah Sussman, Ann Toebbe, Priya Varadachary, Shaun Wright. **Apprentices:** Josh Aiello, Becky Cole